Maureen Freely, journalist for the *Guardian*, *Independent* and *Observer*, author of novels and non-fiction, is the mother of four and stepmother of two. She lives in Bath.

THE

Parent
Trap

*Children, Families and
the New Morality*

MAUREEN FREELY

A *Virago* Book

First published by Virago Press 2000

Copyright © Maureen Freely 2000

The moral right of the author has been asserted

A CIP catalogue record for this book is available from
the British Library

ISBN 1 86049 702 0

Typeset in Berkeley by M Rules
Printed and bound in Great Britain by
Clays Ltd, St Ives plc

Virago Press
A Division of
Little, Brown and Company (UK)
Brettenham House
Lancaster Place
London WC2E 7EN

To Lennie Goodings –
this book's other parent

Contents

Introduction

The story so far

I've been a parent for twenty-one years. During that time, there have been only four years when I didn't have at least one child who was under five. I can't remember the last time I walked out of the house without first asking myself, 'Will I see enough of my children today? Who is going to look after them while I'm away?' There has not been a day when I was not surrounded by other parents asking themselves the same questions. But all this caring and arranging has happened in a strange sort of underworld about which people in public life were ignorant, dismissive and incurious.

Until very, very recently (more about that in a moment), parents counted for nothing in the world of politics. In the world of work, our ratings were not much higher. We did not suffer from outright discrimination, because employers took us on in great numbers and were prepared, for the most part, to keep their minds open about us . . .

. . . But only so long as we did not refer directly to our tragic flaws, our children. Anyone who forgot that rule was quickly dismissed as not very serious. Anyone who persisted caused first surprise, then impatience, and finally the kind of exasperation you or I might feel if we went to a restaurant and got stuck with a waiter who insisted on telling us all the ingredients in every last dish, and went on to spell out exactly what the chef planned to do with them, without realising we only really cared about the end product.

That was all the great and the good seemed to care about when it came to child-rearing – the end product. Their specifications for the ideal model were vague, but suggested a well-groomed eighteen-year-old who knew how to say 'please' and 'thank you' and could probably be trusted with heavy machinery. They were never quite sure how one went about creating such a triumph – but that, many thought, was just as it should be. Ideal parents were by definition elusive figures who lived to serve and never signed their works.

This left the genuine articles with little room for manoeuvre. There was no way to call into question the general treatment of parents without also calling your own credentials as a parent into question. The only way to escape censure was to draw attention away from yourself, agree to do your caring and arranging invisibly, without making demands or ever complaining about your lot. Colluding, in other words. But you didn't have much choice.

The strain of keeping up this façade was considerable, especially for those of us who felt that our jobs depended on it. In the newspaper offices that have dominated my own life for the past ten years, it was especially irking in times of scandal. Whenever someone somewhere killed a child, stole a child, left a child alone, had too many children, pioneered a new kind of fertility treatment, got divorced, chose to become a single parent, or even became a single parent by default, our child-blind superiors would pontificate endlessly about the 'Decline of the Family' or the 'End of Childhood' or 'Selfish Parents Who Work Until All Hours Just So That They Can Drive Around in a Souped-Up Audi'. The more removed these people were from the exigencies of childcare, the more qualified they felt to pass judgement; the more irate they were if those end products failed to please.

These people didn't see the problem, because they *were* the problem. But at least my like-suffering friends and I had a quick and easy escape. All we had to do was pick up our briefcases and go home to our children. Who were so much wiser – so much more fun! – than the self-important idiots who could not even see them. What a pleasure it was to throw away our masks and bask in obscurity! This is not to say that we were left entirely to our own devices. We were ringed by doctors and health visitors and teachers who would, we knew, be quick to intrude if they thought we were being cruel or neglectful. But we were hardly going to fault them for that. We knew from experience that so long as we kept within humane limits, the helping professionals would leave us to find our own way.

Invisible, off-stage parenthood was not without its perks and freedoms, which is why so many of us went along with it. But that was then. Today the picture looks rather different.

The picture as it looks today

Almost overnight, the Parent Question has gone from being one of the most boring items on the political agenda to one of the most urgent. It has undergone a media remake, too: family issues that editors either dismissed as 'not newsworthy' or relegated to the parent page ghetto are now matters for important analysts to discuss on comments pages. When

cabinet ministers make statements about children at risk,
fairness at work or parents under stress, they can be pretty
sure they'll make the front page. They no longer have to
spell out the reasons for their concern: we are all aware that
society is failing its children, and failing also to support those
who care for them. We know, too, that our old domestic
arrangements have broken down, and that we need to restore
or replace them. To fail to do either could, we fear, have dire
consequences for our future as a culture. We are only too
aware that today's neglected children could become tomorrow's deficient adults.

How did we come to acknowledge this national emergency? The catalyst was New Labour, the first government in
this country ever to acknowledge that the problems of
modern family life are too big and too important to be left for
individuals to resolve privately. But like all shifts, this one has
been decades in the making. If we look back over the newspapers of the past twenty years, we can see several debates
running in parallel and then converging under the tutelage of
New Labour.

The first debate

The clearest and most dignified of these debates has its primary
home in Westminster, but it also makes regular appearances on
the comments and analysis pages of the quality press. It does
not have a formal title, but if it did, it would be, 'What to do
about the Family?' It arises out of a long and honourable philosophical tradition, in which there are no new ideas but rather
new readings and refinements of Aristotle, Rousseau, Locke,
Hobbes, Engels, Adam Smith. Real families do not get much of
a look in here – except as statistics. Statistics are what give this
debate its growing sense of emergency. It's the statistics on

divorce, illegitimacy, teenage pregnancy, delinquency, crime and urban blight that prove the family is in trouble, can no longer perform its social functions, needs to be saved, improved, supported, warned or admonished.

The people who take part in this debate come from all parts of the political spectrum and have vastly different ideas about why things have gone wrong, and what society can and should do about them. But in other ways they are very much alike. They are mostly male, mostly of a certain age, and mostly in positions of authority. One can only assume that most of them also live in real, modern families. Even so, they hardly ever speak as family men in this debate, but rather as politicians, academics, economists, business leaders, lobbyists, union leaders, social commentators, UN representatives and members of the judiciary. Often they are linked with think tanks, and often it is only a matter of time before their proposals become government policy. When this happens, the outcomes are analysed and assessed by other serious thinkers on other comments pages: most of these people will also go on to influence policy in due course. In the end, it's a very tight little community. The standards these thinkers keep might be high and the rules of engagement strict, but for the same reason there is something rather unreal about their gravitas. There is this pretence that they are discussing problems from which they themselves are exempt; they write as if they are Victorian gentlemen sitting in their studies, deciding what to do about the disorderly and ill-mannered ingrates downstairs.

Perhaps they are nervous because they can hear so much noise coming up the stairwell. And here we come to the second debate. We can see it taking shape – slowly but surely – in the second, lesser world of women's magazines and newspaper features pages.

The second debate

This second, lesser debate is the point of entry for 'the voices from below'. This is where you get a sense of the joys and frustrations, the ethical dilemmas and urgent issues of modern domestic life: the inside story on the crisis in the family. It's in crisis, you hear now, because nothing fits. School schedules don't fit work schedules. Mortgages don't fit houses owned by people who don't have jobs for life. Salaries don't fit childcare costs. Nothing fits families that don't look like families as they were all meant to be in the 1950s.

Despite the lowest common denominator language and the user-friendly formats, we see important things happening as this second story progresses. In the early years there are the fights to take birth control, childbirth and childcare away from the experts: the old monopolies crumble, and soon there is no one left who thinks Dr Spock knows best. As women have more choices, the mood changes. When the first wave of women with children go back to work, the focus is on getting them accepted in the workplace. As the numbers increase, the focus is on getting them a better deal so that they are no longer slaves to that workplace. As the old domestic arrangements disappear, more certainties dissolve and are replaced by turf wars. We see a proliferation of special interest groups: single mothers, stay-at-home mothers, active fathers and fathers who have been denied access to their children, working parents and step-parents. Then there are the other campaigns, not so much by parents for parents but by parents and other concerned parties for children. The campaigns to end bullying and smacking are part of this movement; so, too, are the campaigns to publicise child abuse, to bring all forms of cruelty to children to a full stop, and to promote 'emotional literacy'. With every new movement, so we see a new army of experts and advocates, many of whom are working in fields that didn't even exist twenty years ago – fields like parent education, divorce mediation, early intervention and children's rights.

As time goes on, their concerns are reclassified. They cease to be private issues and become matters of public interest. Once this has happened, you begin to see the parent and child experts bursting out of their features articles and little advice boxes, and venturing over the great divide to address the general public in the serious news section. Here they work hard to highlight the many problems that beset parents and children and that the general public has been neglecting. They outline the work that needs to be done, and they make impassioned pleas for help. The think tanks listen; they invite the new experts over. The new and old experts confer. New ideas emerge, out of which come new laws and new policies. Some of them – like Thatcher's Child Support Act and Major's 'Back to Basics' campaign – backfire and in so doing add to the growing sense of crisis. A government-in-waiting sees the opportunity in this crisis, puts the problems of families and children at the very centre of its manifesto and sweeps into power.

Now suddenly there is plenty of money on offer to the new experts, and lots of new networks and foundations offering plenty of jobs. Because the new government cannot afford to let the new debate on the family live solely within the confines of its own magic circle; it wants to win everyone over to its new, inclusive vision of family life. So now these experts become the government's most important allies. It needs them to deliver the services that are to make this vision a reality, and to convince 'middle England' that they are services worth having. And so we begin to see more and more of these experts going back and forth, back and forth, over the great hard news/soft news divide. One week we'll be reading an article on the comment page in the *Guardian*, in which the director of a new relationship research foundation discusses the policy implications of a new study of demographic indicators of marriage breakdown. The next week, we'll see the same director in *You* magazine, offering useful pointers in an article entitled, 'Seven Signs that Your Marriage is Heading for the Rocks'.

Her aim will be the same wherever she is: to raise awareness of the issues that concern her. But different audiences speak different languages. To get her point across to the serious policy people, she must respect their terms of reference, or else lose their respect. When she addresses the other, 'softer' audience, the people who are living the problem, she must be just as careful. Unless she is warm and personal, and uses real-life examples, unless she avoids the words politics and economics and any other term that smacks of policy-speak, these people will sigh and turn the page.

As she darts back and forth between the two languages, she finds that some of her most urgent concerns become lost in translation. At the front end of the paper, she is forced to be too general and abstract. At the back end, she is forced to be too personal and specific. She can ask the little questions here, but never the big ones that most concern her. As we watch her struggle to find some way to put the two halves of her message together, it becomes clear that her mission is doomed: the very structure of our morning newspaper makes it impossible.

How to put the two halves together?

How would our grassroots activist-turned-expert phrase this message, given an audience that was prepared to listen? We do not need to be entirely hypothetical about this, as such an audience already exists. If we put down our newspapers for the moment, if we peer through the crack between its two halves, we can see the story-that-is-not-yet-a-story, the coming together of the serious people with power and money and the new experts and grassroots activists who are soon to become their official agents.

Imagine them as they so often are these days, in a conference hall that is open to journalists but still, for the most part, ignored by them. On the stage is a cabinet minister, along with representatives from the Lord Chancellor's Department, the Treasury, the Home Office and the Social Exclusion Unit. Sitting alongside them is the director of a family policy think tank, the patron of a distinguished research foundation, the new head of a parenting education network, and the founder of an umbrella organisation that aims to put emotional literacy into the National Curriculum. Most of the 400 people in the audience have links with these and the other parent-run organisations. And there are more government officials here to listen, get focus and take stock.

There is an air of excitement in the room, because everyone there knows they are participating in a historical first. Never before have the public and private worlds come face to face like this. Even five years ago, the thought of all these disparate groups sitting together in one place would have been impossible. Even now, it seems like a miracle. But how to keep the miracle going, that's the question, because the groups in the audience have so many conflicting aims and interests. The single mothers' groups, for example, do not always see eye to eye with the aggrieved men representing fathers who have lost custody of their children. The stay-at-home mothers' groups are suspicious of those representing working mothers, and the feelings are mutual. The non-religious groups are impatient with the religious groups. The pro-marriage associations do not sit easily with the organisations representing step-families. The children's rights groups have their doubts about the parents' rights lobbies,

the organisations of Asian and Afro-Caribbean parents'
groups are dubious about the groups run mostly by whites,
and mostly *for* whites. There are tensions, too, between the
big government cheeses and the little government cheeses.
All these tensions could worsen as the groups begin to com-
pete for all that new money.

At the same time, all in attendance are also aware of a
common agenda. They have gathered together to address a
problem too big to be left to families to solve privately – and
so new, that most people outside this room have yet to
understand 'how big it is'. The old social arrangements for
bringing up children have broken down, and if they cannot
come up with a set of new arrangements, our future as a
society will suffer. The only way forward is for the representatives of the two worlds to meet, to hammer out a new
strategy.

And so here they are, the two halves of the equation, peer-
ing at each other across a divide that once acted as a blind,
and that they are now trying to see as an equals sign.

They have yet to learn to trust each other. To the people on
the government bench, there is not enough professionalism in
the way the grassroots warriors operate; they are worryingly
shambolic, and not as grateful as they should be. To the
people on the grassroots bench, those on the government
side are too locked into formal rules, put too much trust in
top-down policies, and are ignorant about what it's really like
to take care of children.

Each side entertains a distinct set of high hopes. The government people hope that by investing now in families, they
can turn us into a nation of healthy, wealthy, socially responsible obedient and amenable citizens. The parent activists, by
contrast, hope to use the government money to give parents
more power over their own lives and more say in government policy.

Their fears clash, too. The worry on the government side is
that the massive investment in these well-meaning but disorderly organisations will be for nothing. Despite all the money
it is about to pour into parent support and education, the
divorce rate could keep going up, along with the crime rate,
the teenage pregnancy rate and the poverty rate. And who
will look like a fool then? The worry on the parents' side is
that what begins as friendly, open-ended government intervention in family life could end up becoming crude,
moralistic and intrusive. Instead of (to use their own
favourite word) empowering parents, the new deal could end
up being something that polices parents, and punishes them
for departing from the government-condoned norm. . . and
keeps them from having any power at all.

But these fears have a hollow ring when they voice them in
the conference hall. Because there is nothing in this story-
that-is-not-yet-a-story to suggest crude moral judgements or
harsh tactics. All the talk is about richness in diversity, community networks and inclusion. Speeches are carefully
phrased, open-ended, open-minded and polite. All in attendance agree that assumptions and plans for the future must be
based on hard evidence and careful research, must be subject
to scrutiny and revision, must *not* be based on wishful thinking, pretty fairy-tales or narrow moral codes. All shudder to
think how wrong things could go if they allowed fairy tales
and narrow moral codes to intrude at this delicate moment in
the negotiations. But there is little discussion of the third
debate, in which their worst dreams have already come true.

The new morality

This third debate has its primary residence in the tabloids.
Even the quickest review of the last twenty years of tabloids

will show that they were way ahead of the quality papers in defining, fanning and politicising fears about the crisis in the family. They were also way ahead in identifying the stories that best illustrated the problem as they saw it: neither philosophical nor practical but moral. The moral of the story as they told it is that the fabric of society was eroding because women were no longer doing what women were put on earth by God to do, and neither were men. They were parenting unnaturally, and the result was a new generation that was lawless, degenerate and monstrous.

To prove this point over the past twenty years, they have given great and steadily increasing attention to a rogues' gallery of parents who fit the bill. Some entered the limelight through their own ill-advised efforts; but many other parents get the same treatment, and see their stories twisted into scandals, even though they have done nothing except live outside 'the traditional family'. This is the main concern of the editors who are running these campaigns. Every scandal comes with scathing leaders about the evils of divorce, feminism, working motherhood and the welfare state. They all end with the same moral: it is time we went back to stay-at-home motherhood and bread-winning fatherhood, and no sex before marriage – the way we never were.

You could say that this is much of a muchness, that conservative tabloid editors lead inevitably to conservative comments pieces, that they're preaching to the converted and so not very influential. But if you look at the debate in the quality press over the last 20 years, you begin to see that this third debate might be based in the tabloid world but does not confine itself there. Whenever there is a very big scandal involving bad parents or criminal children – the Cleveland child abuse allegations, the Bulger case, the Mandy Allwood saga or the Louise Woodward trial, to name just a few – the dam bursts and the debate is soon flooding into the qualities.

It goes right to the front page and often stays there for weeks and weeks, while also spreading through the paper and dominating both sides of the hard/soft divide. It draws energy from all the serious movements that are concerned with murderous, inadequate and neglectful parents. Children's rights campaigners frequently find the need to add their comments. So do child abuse experts, juvenile offending teams and charities concerned with children's mental health. As the picture darkens and the entire country gets drawn into the panic, the Home Secretary passes judgement, and so does the Prime Minister. They are not just giving sound-bytes; they are shaken by these scandals too. Looking at the progression of scandals over the past ten years shows what a powerful effect they've had on government policy – and also on the rest of us. The string of moral panics has become central to the public understanding of what is wrong with families today, and what needs to be done about them.

As a nation we have become obsessed with fears about damaged children and endangered childhood. Such feelings are perhaps natural in a time like ours, when we're grappling with such rapid social change. Fears are most frightening when we can't put names and faces to them, which perhaps is why we are so eager to turn our attention away from our own children – who might be damaged, and who could be endangered – to those who already carry scars. In this sense, our newspapers are not inventing our moral panic about parents, children and childhood, but rather providing us with the stories that give our panic substance.

Because these stories come and go so fast, because we are either up in arms about them one day and then, a few days later, not even thinking about them at all, it is hard to see what effect they have on our thinking in the long term. But if we put all the stories of the past twenty years back to back, we can see our suspicions about parental standards being confirmed almost daily by the dreadful stories about deranged baby-snatchers and killer babysitters, mothers who leave their children home alone and go off for a fortnight in Benidorm, and mothers who stay at home while their boyfriends beat their children to death. Everywhere we look we see paedophiles. Some run children's homes, others run scout clubs or masquerade as teachers, priests, doctors, nursery aides and counsellors. Many are stepfathers. Biological fathers have a record that is only slightly cleaner and, while most mothers continue to be above suspicion, the endless procession of scandals featuring abusive and murderous mothers is slowly undermining our complacency.

Faced with this endless procession of disgraced, failed and criminal parents, it is hard even to think about procreation as a basic human right. In fact, it *is* a human right (article 12 of the Human Rights Act that became law here in 1998 is the right to marry and found a family). But every time we read of a child who has been hurt or abandoned, abused or killed, we cannot help but ask, how did we let this happen? Why were these parents entrusted with this fragile, innocent life? Why didn't social services see what was coming, and place the child in a safe and loving foster home? The same questions come up whenever we hear about 'inappropriate' men and women receiving fertility treatment. Aren't there enough children suffering at the hands of inadequate parents already? It is crazy, we say, that we are aiding and abetting such individuals to have more children than they can handle. Parenthood, many are coming to believe, should not be an option that is open to just anyone. We cannot hope to eradicate cruelty to children, more and more people are saying, unless we limit access to fertility and make sure that all successful applicants attain the proper level of proficiency.

The idea that parents need to be improved morally, and

held to strict public standards, is one that is gaining support right across the political spectrum. Returning briefly to the story-that-is-not-yet-a-story, you can see that even here, in this conference hall packed with polite, diversity-respecting government officials and the parent-championing activists, the issue of the 'parent with serious problems' looms very large. The scene brings to mind a teacher who knows all her pupils need her, but who finds herself paying most of her attention to the tiny minority who are trouble-makers.

Elsewhere, sentiments are less refined and the tiny minority is made to look like a large menace. Thus, we have not just right-wing think tanks but also not-so-right-wing think tanks publishing report after report on the endangered family, the inadequate parent and the lawless child. We have the government attributing an ever-expanding range of social ills to parental neglect, abuse or 'lack of preparedness'. There is wide debate about the damage done to children by parents who divorce, or who spend too little time at home because they work too hard, and by parents who ought to have realised that they were too poor, immature and irresponsible to give their children that all-important good start. There is a growing consensus that something must be done to stop these parents in their tracks.

If I am objecting to this line, am I saying that parents should be allowed to do whatever they want, no matter what effect this has on their children? That they need not take responsibility for their mistakes? No, of course I am not. I think it's essential for parents to take responsibility for their children, and for the way they bring them up. As adults, they are accountable for what they do. There may be a limit to what individual parents *can* do for their children, but (in my view) all parents owe it to their children to work with what they have. Even when their lives are constrained and their choices severely limited, they still have a great deal of power over their children, and their children depend on them to use that power wisely.

My problem with the 'new morality' which I have seen developing, scandal by scandal, over the past two decades, is its ambivalence about parents having any power at all. Traditional morality divided parents along gender lines, giving ultimate authority to the male head of household. The new morality sets out to be gender-blind, but it still divides parents into two groups, only one of which it sees as capable of exercising parental power and authority. It would like to demote the other, less 'responsible' parents to the status of children, or should I say, to the status formerly accorded to women before we got the vote.

The parent trap

It was Simone de Beauvoir who first identified maternity as the fastest way for a woman to lose her chance for an independent life. Fifty years on, the concept of the home as a trap continues to be a popular one. So, too, is the idea that a woman with children can escape that trap and retain her independence by holding down a 'real job'. It is just as commonplace to hear women who have 'one foot in each world' complain that they *still* feel trapped: it is less common to hear about the ways in which men who take on traditional maternal duties find themselves similarly compromised. There has been little effort to define how the parent trap has changed over the years. Most contemporary discussions of the trap are about how to escape it or how to cope with it, not about how it's changed. But it *has* changed: the game has new 'rules' and, although they impact differently on different types of men and women, they entrap us all.

In my view, no good will come from parents in traps. I

believe that there are other, more enlightened ways of caring for our society's carers and making sure they do their caring in a humane way.

Central to my own position is the belief that no parent can hope to care for her children in a humane way if she is entirely selfless, or perfectly content to let others set the rules by which they live. For example, I cannot claim to be doing the best for my children if the first thing I do is defer in all matters to higher authority. I shall not be able to do much for them if I agree to stay at home and cultivate my own parent trap.

My children don't only need me at home: they need me to defend their interests outside it – not just their present but also their future interests. And not only their personal interests, but those of their generation. There are serious problems with the way we bring up children today, and the only people who come close to understanding them are those who grapple with them every day of their lives because they themselves *are* parents. If parents do not take part in the public discussions of these problems, if we are content to pass them on blindly to the next generation, they are bound to get even worse. But if we do participate in the debate about family life, we have a chance of solving at least a few of them.

The new morality actively discourages such a debate – first by disqualifying a large number of parents on the grounds that they are 'inadequate', 'unprepared', 'irresponsible' or just plain lazy, and second by setting such unrealistic standards for 'good' parenting that even very caring and responsible parents feel like failures, and watch what they say in public lest someone find them out. It sustains these positions with moral myths that have little basis in reality. I hope that, by showing the gap between fact and moral fiction, I can create a space for a debate about parents that is no longer in thrall to these fictions. Without such a space, we will never be able to come up with the new social arrangements we need so badly.

My purpose

My purpose is first to look at the debates on parents, families and children as they have played themselves out in our newspapers over the last two decades. Most space goes to the debates that have commanded the most attention – the scandals which have fuelled and shaped what I call the new morality. I shall look first at the popular panics that illustrate the threats to decent, law-abiding parents, innocent children and traditional family life. Then I'll try to show the plots they use, the morals that we are encouraged to draw from them about good and bad parents.

However, I need to make it very clear that I am not trying to say parents should never be judged, or to suggest that parents should have total freedom to do whatever they want with their children. I am not proposing that we think of negligent or abusive parents as victims. At the end of the day, they must be held responsible for what they have done.

The same rules apply in my second section, which zeros in on the stock characters that feature in the popular debate about the family. My aim will be to show that they also exert a large influence over even the most innovative serious thinking on modern family life.

In the third section, I'll consider two of the most serious problems facing modern families – abuse and family breakdown – and show how neither the popular nor the serious debates can quite manage to address them. What they do instead is devise strategies to 'prevent' them.

Taken together, these strategies form the backbone of what I call the new morality. In the last section of the book, I chart the evolution of this new morality; then I map out what I see to be its gaps, blind spots and fatal flaws. In the final pages, I make a bold attempt to address these problems. At the centre of my proposed solution is a 'bill of rights' for parents. Like

Cherie Blair's campaign for parents' rights, it is concerned with childcare and workplace rights. But it is very much broader, as it covers parents' activities not just as carers of children and workers and managers of families but as citizens. This awareness of parents as constituting a large and important *public* group, with a vital part to play in the policies that shape modern family life, is crucial. Until and unless parents are subjects as well as objects in that debate, the search for solutions will be superficial and therefore doomed.

My bill of rights therefore combines domestic rights – such as the right to raise children and to plan, choose, share and define the way we care for them – with political rights – for example, the right to represent our children's interests in the public arena, and to explore the ethical and political dilemmas of domestic life in the political arena. I offer this as the basis for a new morality.

1
The Basic Plots

The appeal of panics

This section looks at four stories that helped to convince many people in this country that: (a) babies and young children live under constant threat of abduction; (b) babies and young children whose mothers work also live under constant threat of battery and murder; (c) things are only bound to get worse, because our government is allowing and sometimes even encouraging the wrong people to have children, while actively obstructing those who should be having them instead.

These fears about moral and mortal danger long predate the stories. The stories became headlines because they gave those fears substance, because they allowed people some distance from their fears, and because they made the anxieties more manageable by giving them a narrative shape. ('*This* is what happens if . . .') The stories provided people with a chance to talk about their private fears in the public arena, to puzzle out the causes, point out the effects and propose possible cures. Although the discussions the events provoked were ragged and often less than enlightening, together they gave weight to the idea that traditional values were in trouble, that we lived in a society which had become too laissez-faire about the regulating of family life. They justified the call for tighter regulation that better reflected our 'core moral values'.

In other words, they were very important stories. So it is essential that they be balanced, representative and grounded in fact. But as we shall see, the factual content is low. The stories exaggerate some problems while ignoring others, and they are not representative. To a large degree, our panic about the family is not based on evidence that would stand up in court.

Everyone knows this at one level or another. Yet the desire to believe and find great significance in these stories remains powerful. Why? What is it about these stories that turned them into national sagas? What do they do for us that a more responsible and balanced story with less appealing characters and less dramatic twists could never hope to offer?

In my view, such panics are the modern-day equivalents of medieval morality plays – those hugely popular dramas that illustrated Christian ideas about good and evil, damnation and redemption, in a way that made them 'real'. They offered up sin and virtue in human forms. They provided a blueprint for the good life, and they mapped the road to hell. The sinners in these morality plays gave double value – they were far more entertaining than their virtuous opposites, but they came to sorry ends which reminded the audience that they followed in the sinners' footsteps at their peril. Morality plays were the means by which the church and the people negotiated a moral consensus.

Our modern-day panics operate by much the same rules.

Baby-snatchers

Abbie Humphries was not the first baby to be snatched from a maternity hospital during the 1990s, and she was not the last. If her abduction became a cause for grave national concern, it was partly because there had already been so many other well-publicised cases leading up to it. There was two-day-old Charlie Waylen, who was taken from the Royal United Hospital in Bath earlier that same year, and Natalie Horrel who was snatched outside a Cardiff supermarket. Most famously, there was Alexandra Griffiths, who was snatched from St Thomas's in London in 1990 and not found for seventeen days. When Alexandra's mother, Dawn, first heard about Abbie, she was furious. 'Have they learned nothing from what happened to me?'[1] This, she implied (and the newspapers confirmed) was a country that could not protect its children. When hoax callers tripped up the police investigation later that week, the verdict was harsher. Britain was not just a careless country but a sick one.

It was impossible to look at the photograph of Mrs Humphries with her newborn, soon-to-be-snatched daughter without seeing motherhood disarmed. Writing in the *Daily Mail*,[2] Rachel Billington suggested that the story had touched a nerve because 'it offended against a law of nature which tells us a baby belongs to her mother'.There was a larger concern, too: 'Here was an ordinary, healthy baby girl born to an ordinary happy couple who came to represent the simplicity that we sometimes seem to have lost . . . They seemed as if they might have made up that unit so much agonised over at the moment – a family. What has come to be called a traditional family. When the new baby was torn away we all felt injury.'

She was not the only commentator to use the word injury in this rather curious way and, like the others, she saw no need to explain what she meant by it. But she was keen to make it clear that when she said 'we' she was referring to men as well as women. It was, she thought, a good sign that men were as affected by the case as women were; their 'emotional reaction . . . should give hope and encouragement to all those who feel they are living in a society which has lost sight of their importance.'[3] And indeed it was this sense of emotional unity that all reports stressed when discussing Abbie's distraught parents.

Something else everyone agreed on was that the baby-snatcher's timing could not have been more vicious. Abbie's birth four hours earlier had 'fulfilled a dream for Mr and Mrs Humphries. They already had a 3-year-old son, Charlie, and longed for a girl to make their family complete.'[4]

Note the use of the word 'complete', because it will recur again and again. Look carefully at the perfect pictures of complete families, because they will, too. In real life, our families are never complete. They're never even distinct units. Even the most stable of families are changing in size and shape all the time. All households travel through stages. First they must establish themselves – as when newlyweds set up house together. Then they go through a period of expansion – the phase the Humphries had thought they completed when Abbie was born. But the whole point of having children is raising them to be strong enough to go out into the world and set up households of their own. After the children have grown and left home, a household dwindles and finally disappears when the parents are taken in by relatives, or move into sheltered housing, or pass away.[5]

We are all only too aware of these patterns because they shape our lives, but when we think about 'the family' – even when 'the family' in question is our own – we have a way of flattening and freezing time. All the world over, we turn our family aspirations into pictures of what A.F. Robertson, anthropologist and author of *Beyond the Family*, calls the 'apical norm'. He has found that whenever he asks people about their family ideals, 'they offer an essentially static image of the household at the peak of its achievements, a little portrait of the happy, fulfilled family at its most expanded and extended stage'. This picture serves, he believes, as a 'target for growth'. As such, it works. There are good reasons why people do not idealise earlier or later stages of the domestic cycle in the same way. The building up of a family affords great pleasure, and often seems to make our dreams come true, whereas the 'fission' years can be much closer to warfare.[6]

But even during a family's fission years, we practise the art of photography very carefully. Just how carefully becomes clear when we look at art photography that breaks the rules. Take a modern classic, Dick Blau's 'Family Scene', which features a family sunbathing on a dock. The two fatigued adults are trying but failing to get some peace; they 'seem to have given up, hands over their eyes, slumped and weary', says Anne Higonnet when she describes the photograph in *Pictures of Innocence*. 'Two children plod on, both moving blindly in the same direction, their rhymed movements pushing against the adults' static bulk. The seam of the dock, right in the middle of the foreground, acts as a psychological barrier between the opposed forces of adult and child.' It captures a complex mood that any parent will recognise. The people in the frame are drawn together and repelled by each other in equal measure. But as Anne Higonnet says, 'It is the kind of scene no one would want in their family album, including Blau.'[7] Albums are for the happy times – the births, the weddings, the holidays and the reunions. The rows, illnesses, divorces and funerals get left out.

Newspapers record these sad occasions on a routine basis; but when they picture families that have our sympathy, such as the Humphries, they keep to strict album rules and represent them in such a way as to confirm the values they think they stand for. And the same holds for the reports they write to accompany them.

What the Humphries are like in real life is nobody's business but their own. Their portrayal in the press might be close to the facts or it might be a gross misrepresentation. Even if they were close to our idea of family perfection then, and continue to be so, they cannot possibly be as flat as their press projections.

The press described them (as indeed they describe all 'good' parents who have suffered misfortune) in the same terms we use to describe 'good' parents in a fairy-tale. Like the king and queen in *Sleeping Beauty*, they longed for a child and got their wish, only to have a wicked witch snatch their happiness away. Reports by a couple who may have seen Abbie leaving the hospital stay well within these fairy-tale conventions:[8] Jim and Julie Morris noticed a woman who brought to mind a witch because she 'was walking very quickly and carrying a baby in an odd way . . . really down low against her stomach. She had one hand on its bottom and another on its back but was not cuddling it.' Not a real mother, in other words, but an unnatural interloper. Someone with a 'twisted mind' (as the *Daily Mail* put it[9]) whose desire for a child was not normal but obsessive.

During the fifteen days while Abbie was missing, the public expressed a strong wish not to understand this desire. But some people still tried. Ken Norman of the Portia Trust, which counsels women with obsessive desires to kidnap children, worked overtime to garner some understanding of the affliction. Women who snatched babies were not twisted monsters: they were 'emotionally disturbed and in need of help'. Their obsessive desire tended not to come out of the blue but was usually triggered by the loss of a baby or infertility.[10] Confirming this view the following day, Raj Persaud, media shrink and member of the Royal College of Psychiatry, dared to suggest there was only the thinnest line between twisted baby-snatchers and the rest of us: 'Before anyone concludes that the motivation to steal a child is a sign of severe abnormality, it is important to remember that rescuing children from terrible parents, child abduction and surrogate mothers are common themes in many myths, stories and fairy-tales. These themes suggest yearning for a child is an extremely common fantasy in our culture. What may separate the rest of us from abductors is that their instability and disorganisation mean they cannot obtain a child through a relationship or an adoption agency. Furthermore, their need for a baby is immediate.'[11]

In the case of Julie Kelley, the 22-year-old dental assistant who stole Abbie Humphries, the urgent need to come up with a baby was fuelled not just by a compulsive desire but also by her fear at being caught out in a lie. She had told her boyfriend's parents that she was expecting a baby. They had been delighted and were looking forward to the happy day. According to Helena Kennedy, who later took on her case, Julie had been 'unable to stop the escalator . . . In June the pressure grew. With each passing day the pressure to supply the baby for the nursery became greater.' She had gone to the hospital on that day in July in a 'terrible panic' and had proceeded to present the child to her boyfriend as her own.

Why he believed her is something we cannot know. Why she thought she could get away with it is another mystery. 'While Abbie was with us,' Julie said afterwards, 'I was always under the impression that she was my child and I was devastated when she was taken away from me.'[12]

According to the *Daily Mail*, Julie looked a 'pathetic creature' when she was led to the dock on 18 July. She was 'breathing so fast she was practically gasping for air'. Her forehead was 'furrowed as that of a woman three times her age'.[13] Despite her youth, she looked like a witch. And that, to a large degree, is how people responded to her. Except, that is, for Karen Humphries. 'I had no feelings at all towards the woman,' she told a *Times* reporter several months later. 'I was, and still am, completely indifferent to her.'[14]

But perhaps that is because she thought of Julie as a woman. For the public, she had become more of an unwoman – a negation of everything a woman was meant to be. From the moment she was arrested, Helena Kennedy later said 'some members of the public bayed for her blood'.

Her time in prison afterwards had been a 'horrifying experience' and, although she was 'not a wicked person but a troubled girl that needed help', she had had to live under an assumed name as a fugitive ever since. She was full of remorse, Kennedy said, afraid that her own baby would be taken away from her. Because – strange as it may seem – it turns out that Julie herself was pregnant throughout this saga. After she got caught, she had a 'recurring nightmare' that she would lose her own baby – and that this would be in punishment for what she had done.[15]

Did she get to keep the baby happily ever after? We do not know, and that is a shame. It would be good to know the last act in this story, if only to drive home the point that the mother-child bond is not and never has been sacrosanct. If there is reason to doubt a mother's ability to care for her child, it is neither illegal nor unnatural for the authorities to separate her from the child.

What, then, did the authorities decide in this case? If Julie was truly ill, did she find a cure? Did she arrive at the point where she could take responsibility for her actions and resolve to change?

How much do we need to worry about the larger context – the abduction and child rescue fantasies that Raj Persaud claims are common to all cultures? Not all broody women snatch other people's babies, but the world is full of women who know how it feels to see another woman with a baby when they themselves can't have one. What Julie did may be inexcusable, and abnormal, but can we really say the same thing about everything she felt? We are not likely ever to know, because we don't really want to know. For the public, the story ends when Mr Humphries appears before the cameras to thank the police for their fine rescue effort; his exact words are: 'You have made us so happy. We are a complete family again.'[16]

Undoubtedly Adrian and Bernadette Mooney had a similar dream in mind when they tried to smuggle a baby out of Romania in a picnic basket that same month. Their arrest came only a day before Julie Kelly's. In the eyes of Romanian law, they were stealing the baby and so were little different from the twisted woman who had stolen Abbie. In the eyes of the British press and the British public (and in my eyes, too), the Mooneys' was a silly mistake but a very understandable one. After all, they had adopted another Romanian child a few years earlier. Like the Humphries, they had a family to complete. And it was such a shame to see the infant returned to the grim Bucharest Orphanage No. 1, 'a world apart from the home the Mooneys planned to give her – and not just in terms of creature comforts'.[17]

What a missed opportunity – this poor child could have become one of *us*. To open your heart to a baby is to dream of shaping that baby in your image and therefore, it would follow, your cultural values and your apical norms. And naturally, you want the best for that baby. No matter how it seems to the Romanian authorities, common sense would seem to indicate that a nice home in the London suburbs would have to be an improvement on an orphanage. But in tussles like this, the moral of the story depends on where you locate virtue, and you will locate it in different places according to the culture to which you belong. What *is* constant is the passion for the perfect picture, the family that has just reached completion, the symbolic whole that tells us who we are.

The perfect picture under threat: Diane Blood

Most people would agree that there is a growing gap between our own families and the one implied by this perfect picture. We seem to date the cracks in our real family pictures back to the early 1960s. Before then, we like to think, we all lived in homes with breadwinning fathers and full-time mothers. Our families extended into the community. For example, there was always an auntie down the road to help with the childcare.

Is this picture of lost wholeness accurate? Only for some families, I would say, and only in part. My own early childhood memories, for instance, bear a close resemblance to the perfect picture. My mother was able to stop working as a secretary to care for me and my sister and brother; she returned to work part-time when we were all in full-time schooling. Her mother didn't work either: she belonged to the middle class.

My father's mother, on the other hand, was not middle class and for most of her life she worked as a cleaner. She would have welcomed a few years at home: she couldn't have them because my grandfather did not earn enough as a longshoreman or a trolley driver or a grave-digger, and in any event spent most of the Depression years out of work. Was there an auntie down the road to help out with the childcare? Well, sometimes there was and sometimes there wasn't. My grandmother was an immigrant, and she had to make the

best of many very bad deals. In fact, during the worst years of
the Depression she did hand her children over to her older
sister – who then took them back to Ireland, so my grandmother didn't see them again for years. The family was
eventually reunited, but things were never quite the same as
before.

I would imagine there are stories like these in every family's
history. It is no accident that all the great Greek tragedies are
about families torn apart by rifts and betrayals. But to say
that family life has always been stormy is not to say that today
it isn't stormier than ever before. Because in some ways, it is
stormier. And it is changing shape.

If you look across the industrialised world, it is clear everywhere that the basic ties which held families together in the
past are not what they were. These ties have not changed in
the same way or at the same rate across the board. There are
differences *within* as well as *between* countries, and a marked
difference between what is happening in Northern Europe
and in the countries to the south. But generally speaking,
people are marrying later and having fewer children, and
more of their marriages are breaking down.

More couples live together without bothering to get married, more children spend their lives with just one parent or
spend at least part of their time in step-families, and more
adults live alone. People live longer and, over the course of
those longer lives, they are working less, not just because
they do more part-time, temporary or seasonal work or suffer
periods of unemployment, but also because they spend more
time in education and in retirement.

There are more women in the paid labour force. While it is
true that they generally earn less than men and work mostly
in low-paid or marginal jobs, any time they spend in paid
employment is time they are not devoting to their families.
While no one is sure what effect maternal employment has

had on family life in general, it's broadly agreed that it must have had *some* effect. And if you look at the rise in the numbers of illegitimate children and lone-parent families – especially in Europe and the US, but also to a lesser degree in other parts of the developed world – it becomes clear that getting married and starting a family are no longer one and the same thing. It's not just that more people are choosing to have children outside wedlock. It's also that when they do get married, they no longer commit themselves for life. It's regarded as a contract that you can get out of if you have a change of heart or the other party fails to live up to the terms.

In the law, as in most people's minds, the obligation to a spouse is no longer the same thing as the obligation to a child. But are people really able to meet their obligations to their children without the security and support that a traditional marriage can bring? Although we pose this question whenever and wherever we discuss modern family life, we never ask it quite as urgently as when discussing the new freedoms that have come with reproductive technology.

Abortion, contraception, population control, teenage pregnancy and sex education – they rarely make the news without stirring up concern about the wisdom of leaving women in charge of their own fertility. But nothing makes quite as big a stir as news from the strange new world of assisted conception.

Its ambiguous success stories do not always turn into headlines overnight. Often they are tucked away at the bottom of page 3 or 4. If they move on to the front page the next day, it's because a bishop or a Vatican spokesman has issued a condemnation. A flurry of experts will be called upon for sound-bytes the next day. There will be scattered leaders and comments pieces seeking to make sense of it all, but generally making sense of very little. Then the story will disappear, and it will be as if it never happened – until one day there's another story, about yet another previously unimaginable anomaly.

A 51-year-old woman lies about her age in order to get IVF. A 62-year-old woman gives birth. Another gives birth to a baby from an egg that is partly hers and partly another woman's. Can a child have two biological mothers? A woman gives birth to a child whose father died two years earlier. A virgin gives birth with the sperm of an identified donor. A Neapolitan doctor uses donor sperm without permission only to discover that it's carrying a hereditary disease. An American doctor donates *his* sperm to upwards of one hundred patients.

In California, a child remains a legal orphan while five potential parents – the egg donor, the sperm donor, the surrogate, and the divorcing couple who first 'ordered up' the child – fight it out in court. Meanwhile, back in this country, divorcing couples argue over frozen embryos. The government orders the defrosting of all frozen embryos over five years of age. There is concern in the tabloid press about the number of women using artificial insemination who are single mothers. Then the worry is about the number of IVF users who are lesbians. A doctor is reprimanded after blabbing the truth to a group of children who didn't know they were IVF. A health authority receives the full tabloid treatment after it emerges that it has promised a woman IVF even though the intended father of the child is serving a three-year sentence in prison.[18]

There's outrage, too, when a clinic offers couples help with sex selection. There are dark reports of 'other countries' in which this technology could be abused, and editorials warning that it would cause irreparable damage to society even here. It's the exchange of money that seems to bother people more than anything else. When Gillian and Neil Clark, who already have two boys, pay £650 for treatment that might increase the chances of their third child being a daughter, the headline is: The Rush to 'Buy' a Baby Girl.[19]

The stranger the stories become, the more familiar the drumbeat. There's a growing concern about the kind of people who have been allowed to take advantage of the new technologies. Most are seen as overreaching, irresponsible, unseemly and greedy. 'What is the world coming to?' people ask. It's the same question when we hear about Dolly the cloned sheep, and when we're told that in a few years' time we'll be able to design our own babies. What cock-ups will there be *this* time? What monsters are we letting ourselves in for? Two conflicting nightmares vie for our attention: one features a Master Race, the other Frankenstein. We can't seem to decide which is worse – a world where scientists enforce their desperately impoverished standards of perfection, or where they have the freedom to take stupid risks and produce a race of monsters. Both dystopias carry the same warning: fertility can be a dangerous force when it gets into the wrong hands. And according to many people, it already is.

Their concern is not just that fertility doctors and their patients are defying what anthropologists call apical norms. It's also that they attach little importance to 'procedural norms', what the anthropologist A.F. Roberston calls the cultural consensus governing 'matters of good timing'.

The concern about 'matters of good timing' is common, Robertson says, just about universal. The rules themselves might change from society to society, but all the world over, people 'lose esteem for not doing things promptly (getting married and having a baby) and for doing them in the wrong order (having a baby and getting married). Most societies have some pretty tough ideas about such things as how you get to be a "mother".' There are stages you are supposed to pass through, and you're meant to pass through them in the right order. Marriage might be the most important stage, but it is far from being the only one. It also matters very much how old you are.[20] This is as true in our own society as any other, and it goes some way to explaining both our growing concern about teenage pregnancy and the outrage that people feel about post-menopausal maternity.

Doctors and government officials who are under attack for helping the wrong women to get pregnant routinely dismiss their opponents as irrational – but consider this. Consider the possibility that even the best doctors and most caring bureaucrats – those who weigh their decisions with care, compassion and humility, and are just as haunted as the rest of us by nightmares featuring monsters and master races – might be missing the point simply because they subscribe to the narrow, impoverished, modern understanding of reproduction, the one that sees it as concerning only pregnancy and birth and that classifies the decisions surrounding birth and pregnancy as 'private'.

Their main mistake, according to Robertson, is to talk about families as if they were 'social bricks, static and durable, each brick pretty much like any other in the social edifice' and part of the edifice to perform specific domestic services for society as a whole. This is to ignore what he calls reproductive dynamism: 'As individuals, our own reproductive interests are clearly not confined within the household, but extend to any economic, political, religious or other institution that helps or hinders us in those vital tasks.'[21] Thus I have schools, medical services and building societies to help me bring up my children: according to Robertson, the compact family could not exist unless it had managed to offload much of the work of reproduction onto this web of supporting institutions.

Reproduction, the work that goes into creating the next generation, is not and never has been just a family matter. Everyone and everything is involved. Reproduction 'is a relentless force in our lives, adding and subtracting from the people around us and obliging us to change our relationships with each other and the wider world. It is a persistent strategic challenge, the outcome of which is as important for society as for the persons in each household.'

Reproduction, he goes on to say, is 'simply too important to be left to the whims and fancies of individuals. If each of us is to make a success of reproduction, and if we are to be prevented from allowing our own reproductive adventures to wreck other people's lives, we must take heed of the wisdom which preceding generations have laid down in the form of cultural norms and values. It is a measure of the wide-ranging implications of reproduction that these ideas and ideals reach out to us in every corner of our lives, bombarding us with advice about how the game should be played.'[22]

Seen in this light, the simmering public doubts about reproductive technology are less irrational, and the fairy-tale logic begins to reveal its meaning. As Robertson says, the '"rationale" of child-raising is set about with complex, qualitative issues which are not readily amenable to individual calculation, and instead become lodged in the "folk wisdom" of a culture.'[23] In other words, folk wisdom might be inherently (and unjustifiably) suspicious of scientific progress, and it might be inherently conservative. It might place undue faith in family structures that many of us in the modern world believe to be outdated, but at the same time it might be also be imbued with a vast and complex understanding of a society's reproductive strategies that puts our narrow modern attitudes to shame. It might only be able to express itself in allegories and symbols and put too much faith in perfect pictures, but its concern about the lack of coherence in our present 'reproductive strategy' has some basis.

Certainly this is the moral which most of our qualities and tabloids drew from the story of Diane Blood's long battle to have a child using her deceased husband's sperm. After so many stories about unsuitable candidates for fertility treatment who got just what they wanted, here finally was a decent, sensible woman who had led an exemplary life and suffered the tragic early loss of her beloved husband. Now all she wanted was to have his baby, so why, the papers asked, was the Human Fertilisation and Embryo Authority standing in her way?

If what she wanted was against the rules, then there had to be something wrong with the rules, because she had followed all those procedural norms faithfully. She had married before considering starting a family; she had fully intended to bring that child into a two-parent family, and she and her husband had been discussing the matter in the measured, responsible way we're all meant to do. Once, when they were talking about a woman in the news who'd had a baby by being inseminated with her late husband's sperm, Stephen Blood had said that that was what he wanted Diane to do if it ever came down to it. It did come down to that, and very suddenly, when Stephen was dying of meningitis. Diane persuaded doctors to remove some sperm from his body while he was unconscious. But the HFEA later blocked the use of it as (unlike the husband in the other, earlier case) Stephen had not been in a condition to give consent. But because Diane Blood 'looked right', and because her story 'felt right', the public was on her side throughout her struggle with the HFEA. It rejoiced when she finally got permission to take the sperm ('my precious legacy') to another country, and rejoiced again when she was able to conceive.[24] Another, less prepossessing woman would have been taken to town for doing what she had to do to get sperm out of a dying man in a coma. She would have been accused of wanton disregard for his feelings, and boundless greed. But because she fitted our idea of what a mother should be and look like, almost everyone took her side.

It was left to Libby Purves of *The Times* to wonder what this story told us about our attitudes towards men. 'For all the social prestige of the male, sperm get very little respect. Reverse the genders, and it is hard to imagine a man getting similar sympathy if he asked doctors to cut open his unconscious wife and whip out her eggs.' Anything was possible, she said, if we continued to go down this route. She went on to blame 'the moral relativism of our age'. We did not, she thought, have enough common moral values left to address the ethical dilemmas thrown up by these fertility questions.[25]

And perhaps she was right. But in another sense, Diane Blood is herself a symbol of all the moral values we still *do* share – about men and husbands, as about women and mothers. Indeed, the headlines she gets when she does finally give birth underline the traditional. 'Diane Blood tells of her joy.' That's *The Times*. 'My only battle now is to make sure my baby is healthy, says Diane Blood.' That's the *Daily Mail*. 'Newborn baby boy given life by frozen sperm is the "image of his dead father".' That's the *Observer*; in the picture above it, there is a photograph of rejoicing relatives and a wedding picture. When Diane Blood appears the following Tuesday, there's a photograph showing her clutching an early Christmas present, a stuffed deer called Rudolph. In the *Daily Mail*, there's also a small oval-shaped photograph of her deceased husband with the caption 'Father Stephen: legacy of joy'.[26] Everything confirms that this baby will be moving into a reliable and familiar web of family ties. He will not just look like his father: his mother and his grandparents will make sure he grows up to think and act like him, too. This is what people thought when they looked at the picture of

Diane Blood, radiant new mother, and this was why they were so eager to wish her all the best.

They thought the very same thing, but with a great deal of horror, when they saw that first picture of Mandy Allwood, radiant mother-to-be-of-eight, posing under a tree with her lover Paul Hudson, who was looking very proud, very handsome and very black.

Mandy Allwood: not a suitable case for treatment

Did it really make a difference that the father of Mandy's babies wasn't white? We'll never know for sure. There was no open expression of racism during the seven weeks the Mandy Allwood saga ran. Most discussion centred on the couple's suitability as parents. Mandy was a divorced, single mother; Paul was a bankrupt who had two children by another woman with whom he was still involved. To introduce eight babies into that sort of household, if you could call it a household, was madness. All other considerations paled next to this one. But Paul Hudson later said he had always known they were pressing other buttons too: 'What they said in America was, we like your story because it has everything – scandal, the race card, the womanising, the medical thing, and what's best of all, you're both good-looking!'[27]

One factor he forgot to mention: their choice of publicist. It fell to Max Clifford to make sure the story got the attention it deserved – and didn't he do a good job of *that*! The original story was perfectly positioned to get up the maximum number of noses. 'I'M GOING TO HAVE ALL 8 BABIES,' were the headlines on the first day. It came complete with that picture of Mandy and Paul in three-quarter poses with their arms draped lovingly around the telltale bump.[28]

And oh, how shameless they were about the mess they had

got themselves into. They seemed to see no reason why Mandy should not have been popping fertility drugs.* They apologised for nothing! Not even that tumble on the sitting-room floor that had started it all! 'He little realised that he was making history as well as love . . .' gushed the *News of the World* as it glossed over the details. It was once over lightly again when it came to the couple's decision not to reduce the pregnancy to twins or triplets.

Selective reduction was 'too horrific to contemplate', Paul was quoted as saying. 'Our eight babies were meant to be . . . We're on the edge of science and we're looking for an entry in the *Guinness Book of Records*.' Mandy was quoted as saying: 'I'm deliriously happy. I want nature to take its course. I know that some people will call us irresponsible, but as far as I'm concerned, the more the merrier.'[29]

Later on in the scandal, when asked to comment on her doctor's warning that she was more likely to win the lottery than she was to see all eight babies live, her response was, 'Yes, but people win the lottery every week!'[30] Her mood was so upbeat you might have thought she had already won it.

She tried hard, though, to convince the public that they had not sold their story for base commercial motives. All she and Paul wanted, she said, was to have a little nest-egg so that they could look after their large family, if it ever arrived. There were other small attempts at *gravitas*. As, for example, when the *News of the World* published the ultrasound pictures of all eight babies. 'We conceived our children for love, not money,' she claims in the accompanying article. 'I challenge anyone to look at them and choose which ones should die.' But the ultrasound pictures are blurs in the background. What catches the eye first is Mandy, smiling oh-so-nicely for the

---

*In fact, she was not. She was receiving treatment for a condition called polycystic ovary syndrome.

camera. Then there is the rollicking headline – 'ALIVE AND
KICKING!'

It was after this spread that Mandy's doctor made a public
plea for the media circus to stop, so that she might have a
chance to put her feet up and perhaps give the babies a better
chance of survival. He also pleaded with the press to cease
their facile condemnations of the mother. 'Should we insist
that those waiting for fertility treatment first fulfil ten criteria
of perfect parenthood? Ninety-nine per cent of the population
would fail.' But his call for reason attracted little attention.
The story had taken on a life of its own by now. Mandy and
Paul had become international commodities, with a contract
to honour and appointments to keep. In business terms, it
made no sense for the *News of the World* to abandon a story in
which it had made such a big investment. It made no sense
for the other tabloids, either.

The more dirt they could find on Mandy and Paul, the
more they stood to boost their own circulation figures. They
did not have to dig very deep. So soon we knew that
(1) Paul's other 'wife' was not so happy with the way things
had been going lately; (2) Paul's mother felt he had brought
shame on his family; (3) Mandy's parents were paralysed
with shock; (4) Paul had left a previous ex with heavy debts;
(5) another beautiful young woman was claiming he had
tried to pull her in a night-club; (6) both Mandy's and Paul's
business dealings had big question marks around them;
(7) nevertheless both were still driving around in flash cars;
(8) Mandy had recently applied to go on income support –
and was getting the most out of the extra perks that this
privilege implied: for example, not paying for prescriptions.
Hence the *Sun*'s most strident anti-Mandy headline: 'I GOT MY
BABY FREE FROM BOOTS.'[31]

With each new revelation, public anger against Mandy grew.
For once, no one asked if the tabloids might be embroidering

the truth. Most were happy to read their accounts of her life as fact. In the eyes of many members of the public, she had by now ceased to be human. Instead she became the nation's most famous anti-mother, the symbol of fertility run amok. But the most interesting thing about the Mandy Allwood scandal was that the woman herself was not at the centre of it. The majority of people viewed her as an accident that had been waiting to happen: she made them angry because her 'accident' exposed our regulation of fertility as flawed and inadequate.

At the same time it introduced the public to an ethical dilemma for which no one has an answer. In fact, there had been a minor version of this same dilemma only a week before Mandy hit the headlines. This, the first scandal involving a selective reduction, featured a single mother who was expecting twins and had chosen to have her pregnancy reduced to one. Her reason was that she simply did not have the resources to care for them on her own. There was great outrage expressed by most tabloids at her decision. For them, this was a case of a woman taking away a life carelessly, for selfish reasons. The story brought loud objections from the pro-life movement. Some doctors joined in, saying that selective reductions could only be medically justified in pregnancies of three or more. Champions of 'traditional family values' saw the story as an apt illustration of what happened to morality in families headed by lone mothers. There were, of course, people who saw the mother's decision as responsible. Most of her defenders were adamant, too, about her right to make the final decision. But now, only a week later, there was this other case that gave even pro-choice campaigners pause for thought.

Because if it was *always* right for the woman to have the final decision, then surely Mandy had the right to say no to a selective reduction, *no matter what the consequences*. But to defend her right to make that choice was, in this case at least, to appear to condone a woman's right to refuse to consider the consequences of that decision. It could be the same as saying that those eight potential lives were hers to toy with, that no one else had any right to set limits on that game, no matter what the cost.

But if Mandy Allwood was a hard case for the pro-choice people to champion, it was even harder for the pro-life movement. Or rather, the details of her case made it impossible to defend family values while also opposing abortion. If you decided to view her as the sort of woman who had no business starting a family of eight, then you were dangerously close to advocating a selective reduction. But if you said that she was right to say no to a reduction, you came very near to supporting her right to a family that made a nonsense of every traditional value in the book.

Caught in such a complex moral maze, the tabloids could hardly be expected to discuss the rights and wrongs of Mandy Allwood with much coherence. But there was, nonetheless, a logic to what they said and did. The rules of the market reigned supreme. It fell to the *News of the World* to defend its product with the means to hand, which meant taking a pure pro-life stance and holding it. Its main moral spokesperson was Professor Jack Scarisbrook, of the anti-abortion charity Life. Although he did concede that we were looking at a situation that departed from the traditional ideal, he was still adamant that a life was a life was a life. 'Mandy's determination to save all her children is an inspiration for us all,' he proclaimed. 'What a wonderful mother she must be. Maybe these fertility drugs got out of control . . . but still we should be rejoicing. I can't wait to see the picture of the proud mum and her eight bonny babies . . . you will hear the whole nation say, "Aaaah".'[32]

You might have heard him say the same things in the *Daily Mail* or the *Sun*, had either of these papers won the Mandy

Allwood auction. But now that the chips had fallen where they had, it was uncumbent on them to criticise the competition's product. They managed to evade the pro-life-pro-choice quagmire by focusing their wrath on the NHS. 'WHERE is the morality of giving a woman a drug that produces eight babies in her womb without the slightest regard to whether she is a fit person to have one child, let alone 8?' asked the *Sun*. 'WHERE is the proper exercise of medical responsibility in giving her fertility treatment without consulting her partner? Or caring particularly whether they are married or in a stable relationship? . . . WHERE IS THE SENSE in a doctor prescribing a fertility drug to a woman who is on income support, and who will struggle to take proper care of the children? *There isn't any.* It's no good saying social workers will sort out the mess while a fortnightly Giro keeps the kids in shoes and the mum in fags . . .' The ease with which she obtained treatment, the *Sun* said, was 'an insult to all those childless couples who pumped their life savings into paying for treatment that would make their lives whole'.

The greatest insult, according to many newspaper readers, was to their own intelligence. How could these people who were generating the story (and also profiting from it) dare to lecture *anyone* on the subject of morality? This was the question that dominated the spluttering letters pages, not just in the tabloids now but also in the qualities. A few of the culprits were clever enough to try to align themselves with their disgusted readers by echoing their sentiments: as the *Mail on Sunday* put it, 'the circus surrounding the eight embryonic beings conceived by Mandy Allwood is profoundly distressing. There is nothing of which anyone can be proud. It is a story which brings into shocking focus too much that is wrong with our society; the fecklessness, the greed, the breakdown of family life and the growing moral gulf between what science can do and how people behave. Not the least sad aspect of this story is how the fertility treatment for which so many barren women so movingly yearn, is being reduced to a freak show.'[33]

It was, nonetheless, a freak show that this and all the other papers saw through to its bitter and unsurprising end. It was a story no one could be proud of, but equally which no one could get out of their head. Everyone agreed that it proved there was something very wrong happening. But what exactly *was* it?

When I look back at the cuttings, I see plenty of hypocrisy and media game-playing, but I also see genuine fear and confusion. Take the following highly charged leader from the very first days of the story in the *Sun*: 'What kind of world are we living in?' it asks. 'What will be next . . . selective culling of the womb?' Never mind that this writer has just criticised Mandy Allwood for refusing a selective reduction. The worst-case scenario haunting him here is a man-hating feminist dystopia in which 'mothers discovering the sex of unborn babies through ultrasound scans' have an abortion if it is a boy and they would prefer a girl. But he moves right on to conjure up the spectre of Nazi-style eugenics. Then comes a dystopia in which doctors are willing to play genie in the bottle to every passing political ideology: '. . . will we permit scientists to breed a master race where only the strong are allowed to survive? Where black or yellow, or white babies are aborted because of their colour?'

After this comes a vision of a world in which there are no moral controls over fertility and all children are born outside wedlock. This goes against our deepest values, he goes on to say. 'Bringing new life into the world is the most sublime of human abilities. Planning, conceiving, bearing, and nurturing children is why we are all here – as it says in the marriage ceremony, for those who can be bothered to walk down the aisle.' He contrasts the vision of post-marriage social anarchy with that nightmare's opposite, a totalitarian state in which there are no mothers, fathers or even families: 'we are only a step away from the nightmare world of baby-farming – if we don't stop . . . we will reap a bitter harvest.'[34]

Yes, but *which* bitter harvest? No one seems quite sure. It would be easy to dismiss this wild assortment of worst-case scenarios – this is the *Sun*, after all. But underneath the over-heated language is a consistent argument. Despite the fact that each nightmare describes a different sort of interference with fertility, the fact remains that all the nightmares are about ideologically motivated interventions. They depict societies in which families and individuals can no longer decide how and when they can have children, because the state has usurped their power.

You can see the same sentiments in four otherwise very different letters that appeared together in the *Guardian* later that week. For one writer, 'the fact that medicine has "advanced" to such a point where this could happen, without envisaging the consequences . . . the fact that it can be reported quite matter-of-factly without any apparent disquiet, shows how imperceptibly we are sliding towards barbarity.' For another, the proof of our slide towards barbarity is in our allowing fertility treatment for 'serial parenting', instead of saving it for the truly needy. A third letter-writer claims that Mandy's multiple pregnancy was the direct result of Conservative free market policies. The fourth asks, 'Whatever happened to a woman's right to choose? How has what goes on inside a woman's womb become such public property?'[35]

In the old days, when reproductive technology was cruder and more straightforward, a woman exercising her 'right to choose' would have seen herself as fighting against her husband's or her family's right to treat her body as private property. She would have looked to the public domain to

back up her right to control her own body – to the doctors
who gave her the birth control she needed, and to the laws
that made this exchange possible. But now, suddenly, she can
see that the same forces which had first given her the 'right to
choose' can also take that choice away from her. And that, in
some ways, they have already done so.

How did this reversal come about? This is the question
that all four letter-writers were trying to answer. Although
they came to very different conclusions, all described a society in which individuals and families have less and less
control over fertility. The power has passed over to the medical establishment and the state.

However, it was also clear from what doctors and other
experts said to the press that there was no consensus about
how they should exercise that power. The Mandy Allwood
story exposed as many schisms inside the medical profession
as outside it. They were visible even in the most straightforward warnings which some doctors felt compelled to issue
about the dangers of multiple pregnancies. 'Mothers with an
overabundance of maternal feelings may think it would be
nice to have an instant family the size of a nursery class,'
sniffed one medical person writing in to *The Times*. 'Doctors
who have seen the results of some premature deliveries are
less enthusiastic; they know that to conceive eight babies at
once, however good the home background, presents a failure,
not a success.'[36] He did not go on to add that the main reason
more doctors are seeing the results of premature deliveries
than ever before is that other physicians are giving them fertility treatments which increase the likelihood of a multiple
pregnancy.

Other doctors did make that point. And Professor
Scarisbrook took the medical establishment to task for saying
that Mandy's babies were all doomed to die. How dare they
talk with such certainty? Medicine, he said, was an 'indistinct

science'.[37] There was still a chance that the babies would live. He was not as far out as his critics implied at the time: a woman in Texas did give birth to octuplets two years later, and seven of them survived.

But the strangest schism of all was between Professor Scarisbrook and Mandy's doctor, Kypros Nicolaides. The latter never responded directly to the professor's aspersions on 'doctors with scalpels' and neither did Scarisbrook name names; but as Nicolaides was one of the pioneers of selective reduction, he may well have had this man in mind. However, Nicolaides was far from being a 'doctor with a scalpel'. He went out of his way to support Mandy's decision to continue with the pregnancy. As he explained to the *Express*, the choice was hers; like all ethical doctors, he was there to play the genie to his patient's Aladdin.[38]

He went on to confess that he was troubled by some of the work he did. The truth was that he hated performing any kind of termination. 'Every time I do one, I feel like vomiting.' The worst, he said, were the ones he did in the last trimester. These only happened in the case of severe foetal abnormality; but when they were done, he would go home and sleep with the lights on because 'in the dark I keep seeing images of myself coming towards me like some madmen wielding surgical knives.'[39]

Despite his guilt, despite his doubts, he felt morally obligated to carry on working – to continue helping distressed women to come to terms with their doctor-created multiple pregnancies, to help them understand the risk statistics of his uncertain science and to reflect on them carefully, but within the narrowest of time frames. To guide them to the right Hobson's choice, and then to implement that decision in a professional manner, no matter what that decision did to his own head. What does his forbearance say about him? What do his daily dilemmas tell you about the system he works in? What does this tell you about society, about us? These are the questions that broke to the surface during the Mandy Allwood story. Her vaudeville act did little to allow for an enlightened discussion of them; but, more than any other recent case, it did at least cast light on the central problem.

The central problem is that control of fertility is passing out of the private domain and into the public – but without any clear discussion about what this really means. We don't talk about it because we can't make sense of it. We can't make sense of it because we lack a conceptual framework. We can't fall back on the folk wisdom about how best to bring up the next generation, because it makes no sense when translated into the language of politics. We can't fall back on our old ways of negotiating apical and procedural norms, either; they are out of sync with modern life, but they are still very much alive in our hearts. They make us fear and loathe the new public strategies; we can see that they are narrow and short-sighted, and bound to create more problems than they can ever solve. But we have no other strategies to put in their place. We can't agree on a strategy because there is no longer a cultural consensus about who should be having children, who should perhaps not be, who should have the right to decide on such matters, and when and how.

The only time there is anything approaching a consensus is when someone like Mandy Allwood comes along. Then and only then can everyone agree that the future, whatever it turns out to look like, should not look like *this*. If moral panics can concentrate the mind in this way, then they cannot be all bad. But because they deal in symbols, they do not give the concentrated mind much room for manoeuvre. Rather, they serve to confirm traditional fears, traditional values . . . and traditional prejudices.

The nanny trials: part one

Briton 'shook baby to death'. Baby 'shaken to death in rage'. Toddler shaken to death by enraged nanny, jury told. British child minder convicted.

The above headlines come from the *Guardian*, *The Times* and the *Daily Telegraph*.[40] To whom do they refer? Is your answer Louise Woodward? Think again. Here's another clue. None of the above headlines comes from the front page, and the articles from which they arise account for the sum total of the coverage this particular trial got in the news pages of the *Guardian*, *The Times* and the *Daily Telegraph* in May and June 1999.

The name of the defendant is Manjit Kaur Basuta. The holder of a British passport, a long-time Berkshire resident and a qualified midwife, she and her three children went to San Diego in 1989 when her husband took up a job there as a management executive. In the spring of 1999 she was convicted of causing the death of a 13-month-old boy at the nursery she ran from their $750,000 home. The main evidence against her is a statement by her maid, Christina Carillo, who claimed to have witnessed the attack. It later emerged that there was already bad blood between the two as Carillo, an illegal immigrant, believed Basuta intended to report her to the authorities. There is no way of knowing whether or not this was true: what is on record, though, is that she changed her testimony twelve times. The defence alleges that she made a deal with the authorities, so that she would not be deported. A statement from the boy's father, which was not admitted as evidence, states that the boy's mother, from whom the father was separated, had a history of shaking their son.

Like Louise Woodward, Basuta has always maintained her innocence. So why has her case received so little attention in this country? In the (only) feature article on the case (in the *Guardian*) last June, Manjit's younger brother Amarjit Singh was reluctant to say. 'I don't want to believe this was racism. Our father taught us all never to blame our problems on anyone else; but recently I have had doubts. For the first time I am thinking, "Hang on, perhaps there is an agenda out there." And this is something I don't want to admit.' He did, however, admit to being 'disheartened' by the lack of media interest in the case. The difference between the reporting in this case and that of Louise Woodward 'could not have been more pronounced'. Because there had been so little coverage, he thought it was, 'difficult for the public to develop any sympathy for her. And without national coverage it was hard for us to know how to go about campaigning for her.'[41]

Her case was complicated by the fact that she was convicted under the Tyler-Jaeger Act, a new California law which states that anyone convicted of serious child assault must serve at least 25 years. It is a controversial law, which had led some members of the judiciary to express hopes that in her case it would not stand up in court. Throughout the proceedings, Basuta had the full support of the Sikh community, both in this country and in the US.[42] A British woman whose children Basuta once cared for also spoke out in her favour. But that's about it.

Asked to comment on the differences between the two cases, Max Clifford said, 'You can only assume that everyone was convinced she was guilty.' But then he went on to point out that Louise Woodward enjoyed a number of advantages. 'She looked the part in the pictures – young, round-faced and naïve – and there were pictures that showed her in leg irons and shackles. At the same time, the Eappens came across as if they were out for revenge and not justice.' Asked if Basuta's background and appearance might have worked against her, Clifford said yes, absolutely: 'Most editors are not interested in

Asian people. 'If I have four clients and one of them is Asian, I have to work a hundred times harder to get the same amount of coverage for the Asian client. Being Asian is a huge stumbling block – particularly for the tabloids.' Stephen Jakobi, the founder of Fair Trials Abroad, said he often came up against the 'lack of interest' problem when he was trying to get a higher profile for important cases. 'News coverage is geared in favour of good-looking, young, white women. I call it commercial racism – editors do not think minorities sell newspapers.' According to Suresh Grover, coordinator of the National Civil Rights Movement, only .5 per cent of the cases on their books involving Asian individuals ever got any publicity. 'The other 99.5 per cent fall by the wayside – because the Asian community is not seen as something that will fill pages or sell papers. Unless the individual family push the case forward on an almost daily basis, it is a very hard slog to get attention.'[43]

On the day when a somewhat reluctant judge gave her a sentence of 25 years to life, Basuta's family's efforts to raise the profile of her case had some degree of success. There was concerned TV coverage, featuring Basuta's very angry attorney; there were radio interviews in which family members expressed their grief. Most tabloids put the stories on the back page or nowhere at all, but the headline on the front page of the *Mail* was large and said 'Nanny is Jailed for 25 Years'. The subtitle was more ambiguous: 'Tears of Briton who shook baby to death.' There was no photograph of Basuta on the front page: the picture that stood over the continuation on page 2 was almost as small as a stamp. Contrast these with the way the same paper played the news that Louise Woodward had been found guilty: a photograph of the crying teenager and her distraught father, with the headline: 'DON'T LEAVE ME HERE, DAD!'

Is it racist to ignore someone? If so, it's hard to prove, at least in an individual case. This is one area in which bad press is definitely better than no press at all. With bad press, at least you have written evidence. When no one says a word, you just have to guess. This is more or less what the defence attorney had to do in the Basuta case when he accused the jury of reaching an 'emotional verdict with xenophobic over-tones'. Basuta's brother David was also left to guess about the signals he was giving. 'I wear a turban,' he said. 'A lot of the jurors thought I was a Muslim from Iraq.'[44]

In the individual case, it is extremely difficult to prove that you are being judged and misjudged by your appearance. There are so many different factors in each case, and each is unique. But if you put all the court cases reviewed in this book together, you can see patterns emerging. First, there is no faster way to raise the temperature than to report a tragedy in which a child is the victim. Second, the higher the tem-perature, the greater the part prejudice plays in the way the other actors are seen and judged.

Third, you are more likely to capture the heart and confi-dence of the public if you are young, white, middle class and pretty. You are less likely to do so if you're older, if you're not white or middle class, or if you're a foreigner. If you are young and black and male, you can attract huge press coverage if the story suggests you are the villain, but if you are young and black and male and the victim of a crime, your family will have to fight for years before anyone pays the slightest attention.

In a just world, all lives have equal value. In the symbolic world of moral panic, they do not. The greater the distance between you and the dominant cultural ideal, the less likely it is that the public will care about you, the more likely it is that your testimony will not stand in court.

If you are a foreigner, you also run the risk of your testi-mony being misheard and your appearance misread, which is where the Basuta and the Woodward cases converge. Both women were tried in a foreign country, and both their legal teams claimed they were misheard and misread.

It was the fear of xenophobia that first turned Louise Woodward into a *cause célèbre*. Even people who were not assured of her innocence were so concerned about her trial. The intense media interest may have had everything to do with the fact that she was young and white, but the fear was that she would be discriminated against because she was British. This fear was so intense during the later stages of the trial that it crowded out all other considerations.

The nanny trials: part two

Fears for teenage Briton on murder charge; doubts over 'conflict of interest' in au pair case is worrying friends, reports Tunku Varadarajan. Baby's injuries 'may not have been new'. Boston harbours no doubts about au pair's guilt. Pathologist found no evidence of shaking. 'Catalogue of problems' for nanny. Couple relive au pair case death. Sympathetic hearing from thousands on the Net. Village praises 'calm' babysitter. Au pair tells of attempt to revive baby. Au pair risks 'noose or loose' conviction: Tunku Varadarajan reports on a dramatic decision in the trial of the British teenager Louise Woodward, accused of killing a baby.

Village gripped by nightly drama. The jury's still out – and the strain shows. 2:45 a.m.: Au pair found guilty. Louise Woodward sobs as jury delivers verdict. Trial exposes worst traits of US justice – British lawyers accuse prosecutors of mishandling case as proceedings degenerate into a shambles . . .

This is how *The Times* headlined the biggest childcare scandal

of the decade in October 1997.[45] The actual reporting by
Tunku Varadarajan during this, the first of the three acts in
the Louise Woodward Story, was fair-minded and balanced: it
is the not-quite-as-balanced headlines that best reflect the
public mood in Britain at the time. It's Louise, and not the
dead baby, who's on our minds, despite constant efforts on the
part of conscientious adults to correct the implied emotional
injustice. 'We must not forget that there was a baby who died,'
people keep saying. 'We must not be disrespectful to the
Eappen family in its grief.' We must not, but over and over
again, and to our shame, we almost are. As the trial progresses, it becomes extraordinarily difficult to hold a picture
of Matthew Eappen in our heads. The almost-daily photographs of Louise Woodward keep blotting it out.

Her former employers appear less frequently. During the
first act of the play, they figure less as grieving parents than as
dubious employers. Much is made of their conditions of
employment, little of the fact that by American standards,
they are quite normal. How could anyone that age live like
that and *not* snap? people ask. What sort of people *are* the
Eappens, anyway? Even as they fail to understand the culture
in which Louise was working, they fret about the tragic 'I say
tomato, you say tomato' misunderstanding that may have
landed Louise in jail.

This harks back to the day when Matthew Eappen went
into hospital. When Louise was giving her version of her last
hours with Matthew to the state troopers, she told them that
she had 'popped' him on to the bed to change him. In this
country, 'pop' implies gentle, loving, maternal care. In the
US, though, when you 'pop' someone it means you've either
punched him between the eyes or shot him dead with a gun.

It is harder to chart the readings and misreadings of Louise's
image and body language as the first act progresses, but it is
clear that the average American reading is very different from

the average reading here. The Louise that British audiences see on television does seem to resemble the portrait offered up by her friends and relatives in the Cheshire village of Elton. 'Their' Louise is a soft-hearted teenager who loved pop music, excelled in her academic studies and was affectionately nick-named 'Loopy Lou'.[46] It is hard to look at this Louise and imagine that she could have caused injuries which forensic scientists have likened to 'a fall to the ground from two floors above'.[47] This may explain why this fact rarely stands alone in the British press coverage of the trial. Mostly, it appears along-side reports about the expert witnesses for the defence who cast doubt on the origin of Matthew Eappen's wounds.

When it's Louise's turn to take the witness stand, she handles the ordeal with dignity – or so it seems to most people in Britain. 'Understated' is how many describe her performance. 'Polite.' 'Soft-spoken.' 'Respectful.' Hence the alarm when reports emerge about the large numbers of Americans who on the same visual evidence are sure of her guilt. To Americans she looks severe because she doesn't smile, evasive because she shyly averts her eyes. 'You can see it in her face,' is how one Harvard student puts it. 'She's the nanny from hell.' When Tunku Varadarajan puts the same questions to the professional Irishmen at the Green Dragon Tavern, he is forced to hear 'some routine unpleasantness about Ulster' before being told, 'Let's face it, chaps. You think she's innocent just because she's from England.'[48]

For people here, the trial is an object lesson on the perils of cultural bias. But there are many types of bias at play here and the one that gets the most play in the US – especially amongst those Americans who do believe Louise is inno-cent – is the bias against working mothers.[49] For many, the true culprit is not Louise Woodward but Deborah Eappen. As one waitress puts it, 'How could she leave her child in the care of someone she didn't know? OK, she had a job, she was a doctor, she had a good salary. But does she have a baby now? No. I think she shares some responsibility for choosing not to stay at home.'[50]

There is a strong anti-working-mother strain in the pro-Louise camp in Britain, too. 'Was it right,' asks the *Sunday Times*, 'that an inexperienced teenager be left in charge of two small children while their mother went to work?'[51] As if it never happened here! The implication is that working motherhood is just another strange American custom, nothing to do with us at all.

The consternation about some aspects of the US justice system is not quite so disingenuous. Things that British audiences have a hard time understanding: the fact that Louise arrives in court wearing shackles, the new and different rules about evidence, the fact that there is no summing up, the slickness of her legal team headed by Barry Scheck, the man-who-got-OJ-acquitted. Most disturbing is the prime-time interview the Eappens give on CBS while the jury is still out, when the parents' comments could not be more prejudicial. Sunil says, 'There is no doubt in my mind she murdered Matthew. I really wish I could have stopped her.' Deborah Eappen says, 'I hope she doesn't have any children: that she doesn't have that joy.' The trial has only confirmed her belief that Louise is guilty: 'As the trial goes on, the lies have come out. That's all they are. The same believability was what kept her in our house. The same interest in cleaning up her act, and "I really want things to be better," and crying a little when appropriate – all that act, and how much she loved the children – is exactly what fooled us.'[52]

It wouldn't be allowed here. So why do people let it happen there? And why has the judge, Hillier Zobel, agreed to the defence team's bizarre request for a noose-or-loose conviction? This is another thing that would never happen in

Britain. It means that Louise can no longer be found guilty of the lesser charge of manslaughter, but must either be convicted of first-degree murder or found innocent. No one can understand Barry Sheck's game here – but then again, no one can quite believe a jury could find her guilty of murder on the basis of the evidence provided.

So all hell breaks loose when the jury returns with a guilty verdict. This is the first scene of the second act of this saga – and the scene that will remain fixed in the public imagination for the next six months. First Louise breaking down to 'a convulsion of tears'. Then Louise being 'cradled' by her lawyers as she cries, 'I didn't hurt Mattie! I didn't do anything! How could they do this to me? I'm only 19!'[53] It was, wrote Joanna Coles in the *Guardian*, 'the sound of her weeping the previous night, just after the verdict was announced, that will stay as the symbol of this trial'.[54]

The opinion-makers have been holding themselves back during the three-week trial, but now they make up for lost time. A flurry of legal experts is pulled in to explain why it is that Louise would never have been found guilty of murder in Britain. Mark Stephens, senior partner at Stephens Innocent, criticises the judge for hamming it up for the TV cameras, and television for constantly cutting to the grieving parents. The trial, he says, is 'an indication of why we should not have cameras in our courtrooms'.[55]

But that same day, William Rees Mogg says how pleased he is that we all got to see the US injustice system in action. 'One has to ask what might have happened if the Woodward case had not been televised. The initial press publicity, which may well have influenced the jury, had been hostile to the accused.' It was only by watching television that so many people 'came to the conclusion that the prosecution had failed to prove its case'. Without television, few people would have known how weak the prosecution case was.

He goes on to remind us that Britain cannot boast of a brilliant record in this regard in recent years: the Birmingham Six may have been found guilty because their Irish accents made them sound guilty to a British jury. 'In Boston, after the death of a baby, an English accent may have made the au pair seem like an outsider. Few people are wholly free of ethnic identification at times of emotional stress . . . It is healthy that the American people now know how seriously communal sympathies can colour the responses of juries . . . In Britain our juries have similar prejudices; *the difference is that we do not know it*.'[56] (My italics.)

In the *Guardian*, Linda Grant tries to inject a cautious note into the debate in a column entitled, 'Just How Gentle is Our Sex?' It is, she said, Louise's gender that makes it so hard for us to believe she was guilty.[57] In *The Times*, Nigella Lawson expresses doubts about Louise's canonisation-by-unfair-verdict. 'Just imagine if it was the other way round. What if a foreign au pair working over here were found guilty of killing her baby charge, an infant Briton? Somehow it's difficult to believe that the tabloid press would be quite so insistent on pushing the nanny-of-all-our-hearts line.'[58]

Elsewhere, quiet reflection is pushed out to make way for huge headlines. 'UNBELIEVABLE!' fumes the *Sunday Times* on the week of the verdict. 'Jury believed nanny did not murder baby.'[59] On its front page, the *Guardian* says, 'Defence team scorns guilty verdict. Campaign to free Woodward begins.' The headlines inside are: 'A tale of broken lives played out in the camera's harsh glare'; 'Lawyers refuse to give up hope'; 'Spotlight falls on denial of request for transcript'; 'Defiance and disbelief at verdict unite Woodward's home village'; 'State Prison "No place for a girl"'.[60]

In *The Times*, Bronwen Maddox speaks of the trial as a 'cautionary tale on the hidden dangers' to unsuspecting British teenagers 'in the land of lawyers'.[61] There are questions about propriety, and questions about taste when the Eappens release a photograph of Matthew on the life-support machine. Their aim, they say, is to encourage people to refocus, and remember that we are here because this child has died, and not by his own hands. But here, the focus remains very much on the still uncertain fate of our Louise.

In *The Times*, we are assured that not all the cards are stacked against her. The judge, at least, is an Anglophile – 'the result, no doubt, of his time at Oxford as a Rhodes Scholar in the 1950s'.[62] Clearly he learned a thing or two while he was there: he has no time for nonsense or histrionics, they say in praise. You could not say the same for *The Times*' own head-lines: 'Surplus jurors react in anger'; 'Tough times await in cramped jail'. She's going to have to wear jeans and laceless sneakers while she's there, apparently. And she'll only be able to make phone calls to 'ten pre-selected numbers'. She is bound to get a lot of heat from her fellow inmates: in US jails, as in our own, child killers are 'at the bottom of the pecking order'. The headline for the still continuing Elton Saga is, 'We believe in her. She's an innocent.' Next to the article are pictures of the warring parties' 'rival symbols'. Elton has opted for the traditional yellow ribbon, while the Eappenites follow the example of Deborah and wear caterpillar brooches in honour of Matthew's favourite toy, a caterpillar that played, 'You are My Sunshine'. Deborah Eappen gets her headline, too: 'I hope she can face what she's done, and gain forgiveness.' But her wishes are rather undercut by another story about another British au pair who'd had a chance to work at the doomed house, but had decided she'd rather not: 'Briton rejected Eappen job after Matthew's brother bit her.'[63]

The Eappens embark on a frantic publicity tour in a vain attempt to clear their name and stem Woodward-mania. Speaking on 'Larry King Live' about the criticisms people have made of Deborah's working, Sunil says how unfair that is. Don't they realise that Deborah was always rushing home at every opportunity to breastfeed? Speaking on CNN about her vilification in the British press, Deborah Eappen says, 'They want to make someone a villain other than the person responsible for murdering a baby. The idea that – I hate to use a stereotype – a young, soft-spoken, British-accented, intelligent girl could harm your child is terrifying to people.'[64]

The headline inadvertently proves her point: 'Eappens go on TV attack on their British critics.' And the defences of Louise become more strident. The hysteria grows as 'Lawyer tells of faith in Woodward'; 'Thousands converge on village to join yellow ribbon campaign'; and 'Internet site crashes as thousands log on'.[65] The Rigger, that pub in Elton, gets very crowded. There are crowds, too, outside the courthouse in Boston; some carrying slogans that say 'Louise was lynched!' and 'Reverse the verdict!'[66] And then, on 10 November, there is another 'tense silence as the last act of the drama reaches its climax' and Judge Zobel replaces the mandatory life sentence with a sentence for the 279 days Louise has already served. Or, as the headlines put it, a 'Compassionate Conclusion'. 'Louise is Set Free.'[67]

In Elton, it's a carnival atmosphere as supporters sing, 'She's coming home.' Champagne flows. Family and friends scream in delight, cheer, hug each other and burst into tears. Jean Jones, chair of the Louise Woodward Defence Fund, punches the air twice and says, 'We have done it. We have done it!' Next to her the Reverend Ken Davey, who had led special services for Louise at the parish church, starts hopping up and down while outside cars honk horns and 'well-wishers' set off fireworks.

Mrs Jones does take time out to extend her condolences to the Eappen family. 'If I could turn back the clock,' she says, 'and give them back their son, and that Louise had never left the village, I would.' Sandra McCabe, a fellow-campaigner,

makes similar noises. As does Debbie Lator, the mother who
had once employed Louise as a babysitter. 'In all of this let us
not forget the death of Matthew Eappen. I'm a mother too
and I know what it must feel like to lose a son.' But these
respectful sentiments get drowned out by the party romping
we see on the news. And already in the same papers that
carry the full text of the judgement, the long hangover has
begun.[68]

The third act opens with a column by Libby Purves in *The
Times*. 'The Eappens of Boston have, in their time, asked a
great deal,' she says sternly. They asked that a 'cheap, young,
untrained au pair should take long, lonely hours of total
responsibility for a rampaging three-year-old and a young
baby. They asked, in a coldly worded contract, that she
should supervise them with a closeness few mothers
achieve, never turning aside even to do their laundry. Later,
on the far side of tragedy, they asked the world to accept
Louise as a "monster" . . . they asked a court to convict her
not of negligence or manslaughter, but – absurdly, of
murder . . . They asked the world to let them publicly condemn her on a prime-time TV chat show while the jury was
still out . . .'

In the end, the Eappens didn't get the result they wanted.
But now they have made one final request, and this time they
'absolutely must be heard'. This is their request that when
Louise walks free, she does not have the privilege of going
home a hero.

'Not to go back a hero,' Purves muses. 'Now we're talking.
If anything can be done to prevent the deification of Louise
Woodward, it must be.' She gets this initiative off to a prompt
start by blasting the 'strident intolerance about the pub crowd
in Elton, with its yellow ribbons and balloons and its convenient alliance with an au pair agency rightly terrified of an
Eappen lawsuit. Sentimentality and self-interest have merged

into a mob mentality quite seriously nasty. It has been a kind of party: Eltonians say without a trace of irony that it has knitted the village into one big family.'

The celebrations of this 'fake family' had made her ashamed to be British. As did 'the distinguished British writer who ridiculed Matthew's mother for calling her children Chumbermunchken and Butterball "as if they were milk chocolates" '. Some Americans had also behaved badly, she conceded. Particularly distasteful was the placard outside the courthouse saying, 'One less baby, one more Volvo.' 'Deborah Eappen only worked a three-day week, for God's sake,' Purves fumed. 'Both America and Britain have shown a streak of viciousness over this case which takes the breath away.'

It was pure jingoism, she continued. 'There has been an endless media tearfulness about grim American jails, unfeeling American cops, even the "cheap prison clothes" Louise was dressed in, as if an Armani outfit would somehow be fairer. But American justice did not fail: it faltered, that is all. Having righted itself, it falls upon the British public to follow suit. If the fake Elton now tries to 'attempt any kind of hero's welcome, they will be even more sickening. If Louise comes home to sell her story she will truly become the "monster" that her erstwhile employers call her.'

The same day, in the same paper, Nigella Lawson brought the story even closer to home by comparing it with the James Bulger case. 'For Louise, we demanded clemency; for the boys who killed James Bulger, we demand no mercy.'[69] Virtually overnight, almost everyone was responding differently to these clearly partial pictures which we were still getting of Louise every day. Even as she thanked the judge, her supporters and the au pair agency that had been paying her legal bills, and expressed her continuing sadness at Matthew Eappen's death and her hope that scientific evidence would one day reveal the truth, she was forced to address the rumours which had begun to circulate about her having sold her story to the press for large sums. 'I want to set the record straight,' she said. 'I have done no such thing . . .'[70] But could she be believed?

Because now, as Louise sits in Boston awaiting permission to travel home, some very ugly stories have bubbled to the surface. The first is an allegation that the Woodwards forged a receipt for £9,000 while they were (non-paying) guests in the home of a member of their defence team.[71] Another comes from Jean Jones, a founding member of the Louise Woodward Defence Fund; she accuses the Woodwards of being obsessed with money and resigns.[72] Her allegations are still hanging there in mid-air when we hear that the Massachusetts Supreme Court has upheld the manslaughter verdict and Louise is free at last to return to Britain. When she flies home later that week, the bland but chilly headline in *The Times* is: 'Woodward flies home on a first-class ticket.'[73]

Meanwhile, back in Elton, 'chastened villagers' are making arrangements for a 'muted' celebration of Louise's return. The most chastened of them all is Linda Johnson. She takes down the 'Welcome Home Louise' blanket she had hung in her window after others told her it was insensitive to pose for photographs next to it holding her baby. 'It upset them because of Matthew Eappen,' she tells the press. Then she adds, 'I hadn't thought of that'.

It is against this darkening background that 'Woodward does a Di on Panorama'. That's how the *Sun* plays her TV interview with Martin Bashir, and it's not far off. She's wearing the same dark suit; she has the same highlighted hair; her hands are resting on her lap; her lips are pale, her eyes heavily accentuated, just like Diana's. Hmmm. Could this be deliberate? It must be, is the general verdict. But is this so very sinister? Asked Grace Bradberry, 'If you're trying to establish your innocence, you could hardly go for blood-red lips and nails. What were we expecting? A smirking Cruella de Vil looking straight to camera and saying, "I got away with it," before breaking into demonic laughter? Well, yes, in a curious way, that *is* what we were looking for.'

Others, among them Simon Jenkins, still insist that Louise Woodward deserved the benefit of the doubt. But she does not get it: her mask has slipped. This moment in the Woodward saga is almost unique in the recent history of domestic crime cases. The sudden reversal of Louise's media fortunes doesn't make *everyone* stop and think, but a record number of commentators are aware of the plot conventions to which we have been in thrall. For a brief period, the invisible becomes visible. And once the prejudices that turned Louise into a heroine are there for all to see, her defenders turn silent as they consider the horrible possibility that they might have got this one wrong.

What we learned from Louise Woodward

As the media nation looks back over its many months of possibly intemperate reporting, the mood becomes sadder and wiser. Hopes are expressed that there might be lessons we can learn from it. After all, Louise Woodward would never have become an international *cause célèbre* unless her story highlighted so many areas of concern. Innocent or guilty, she has given us a chance to engage in a long-overdue debate, not just on 'the use of cameras in the courtroom, the role of expert witnesses, and even some perceived racial overtones'[74] but also on childcare and working mothers. It's also allowed us to give serious thought to the realities of child abuse – while never forgetting the possibility that there might also be what Harvey Silvergate called 'the cult of child abuse', or rather, the exaggeration of what we all know is a real and serious problem. It has given us a chance, we think, to discuss where the truth ends in such matters and where the embroidery begins, to ask who is really acting in children's best interests and who is motivated 'more by ideology than by science'.[75]

The most important thing we learn is that people are not always as they seem. Martha Coakley, one of the district attorneys involved in the case, put it like this in an interview with *The Times* after the trial was over: 'By and large, people expect criminals to look like criminals. People who are crack addicts look like people who would do those things. But child abuse and domestic violence are very different. People who look like you and me and the mailman, the priest and the babysitter, hurt and kill kids. It makes your world pretty unsafe, doesn't it, when you can't figure out where evil lies?'[76]

This echoes our sentiments here exactly. Just as we are aware that we cannot know from a single appearance on a Panorama programme if Louise Woodward dunnit or not, so too are we aware that, actually, we're pretty bad at reading the clues in our own homes. At the same time, we are reminded of how much trust is involved in the everyday care of children, how many strangers even the most overweening of parents is obliged to depend on during the long years of rearing a child.

And so to the 'obvious' conclusion: we must find a way to tell the difference between good carers and dangerous carers. We must protect our children against potential abusers. So the time has come, says Dr Thomas Stuttaford, to make sure the public is fully aware of shaken baby syndrome.[77] Time, says Tricia Pritchard of the Professional Association of Nursery Nurses, to push for regulation of child carers. 'We must now start lobbying the government to put in regulations to ensure there is not another Louise Woodward around the corner.'[78] Anne Waddington, a barrister who specialises in child protection cases and who also represents Playpen, a charity that campaigns for a national register of child-carers, tells the *Guardian* that the Woodward case 'has highlighted how ill-equipped parents are when it comes to choosing child carers, and the lack of information available to them'.[79]

Too true! As anyone who has had to look for childcare in this country or in the US will have to agree. Childcare provision in both countries is, quite simply, a scandal. But the scandal is far greater than the 'need for tighter controls on babysitters'. To define the problem in this way is not just to encourage paranoia about the killer babysitters in our midst: it is also a cop-out.

Because, after all, the Eappens aren't the only ones, are they? It isn't just 'Over There' that au pairs and untrained teenagers take care of very young children. It happens in Britain too. In spite of the constant harping about how shocking it is that a family 'as affluent as the Eappens' should have left their precious children in the care of an untrained and inexperienced teenager – everyone knows that it's inexperienced teenagers and other untrained parties who do the lion's share of the childcare in this country too. Everyone knows, and everyone is praying to God that no one will mention it.

Dr Mary Selby echoed these sentiments exactly when she wrote a letter to *The Times* defending the Eappens against their critics. 'Let anyone who has never left their child in the care of someone else, even for a moment, condemn them,' she said. 'And let the rest shut up.'[80]

This, in effect, is what we did during the Woodward case. We talked and talked incessantly about every other issue the trial raised, but we kept our mouths shut over the one issue that really touched all our lives. We never heard, for example, that there was only one registered childcare place in this country for every eight children under eight. Or that most families could not even afford these, and so were forced to depend on 'informal' or 'casual' care. Neither did we hear the truth about childcare in the US. Despite all the talk about the 'daycare factories' of America and overworked au pairs, no one saw fit to mention that a large but undocumented percentage of American children – middle-class children as well as those from less privileged backgrounds – are in the care of undocumented workers.

Had this story really helped us 'look at the issues', these facts would have been at the forefront of our minds. Having acknowledged them, we would have had to see the story not as some freak event 'Over There', but something that could have happened to anyone. We would have been less able to blame it all on a floating population of unregulated killer babysitters, and under pressure to admit that actually, due to the sorry state of childcare provision in both countries, many carers were operating under severe strain and many children were therefore at risk.

But that is not the sort of thinking that scandals encourage; it is not what they are there to do. What scandals do is first jolt people with a shock of recognition and then let them off the hook by allowing them to pretend they are only spectators. That is what the Louise Woodward story did: first it scared us half to death, then it let us pack up all our anxieties and send them overseas.

But now that the drama is over and the tempers have cooled, it ought to be possible to go back to the beginning and think about it again, this time with a little more compassion. What really happened in that house during the days before the tragedy? What was it like when it was just a household that was not that different from mine or yours? What was it like to be in Louise Woodward's shoes in those days, and what was it like to be in Deborah Eappen's?

I have thought a lot about both sides of that question over the past three years, because I'm one of the millions of women who have been in both positions. I worked as a mother's help when I was a student – as it happens, not far away from where the Eappens live in Cambridge, Massachusetts. Like Louise, I came from abroad. I was lonely, confused, untrained, inexperienced and 18 years old. Although I gradually grew accustomed to the way this family brought up children (and drew upon it later on, when I had my own) I initially found these methods very bizarre.

Before I did go on to have my own children, I wrote a novel that made much of that bizarreness. Although it was a piece of fiction about a family that did not exist, the plot I devised speaks volumes about my own assignment of family vices and virtues at the time. At the end, the youngest child, a boy, dies – not because of the loving, caring and selfless mother's helper, but through the neglect of the boy's mother who has been distracted by her job and a pending divorce. There is more to the story than I saw when I wrote it. When I read it now, I can see how much it captures of the fraught and complicated relationships in a household where there's a teenager looking after children. She needs the mother's advice and attention, and she's angry when her overworked employer forgets to give her these things. She craves and needs instruction and she resents it. This is partly for babyish reasons and partly because the more attached she becomes to the children, the closer she is to their feelings – especially their feelings about their parents' divorce – and the angrier she grows that no one else seems to care. And the more ideas she has about what she could do to make them feel better, the more she realises that she has no power at all. She remembers that at the end of the day, despite the family's efforts to treat her 'like a member of the family', she is *not* a family member but an employee. All the mother has to do is say, pack your bags and go, and these children are lost to her for ever.

The mother's helper is not imagining all this; her position really is constrained, and therefore hard to bear. But when I read this book now, I can also see how it looks from the mother's point of view. I can understand her fatigue, her divided loyalties and her sometimes ridiculous but always valiant efforts to be all things to all people; her efforts to stabilise others as she herself is almost going under during the divorce. And I can see how it is for her in the larger world, as she shuffles between her children and colleagues who resent her absences every bit as much.

And then those other things she has to undergo every time she needs to 'seek new childcare arrangements'. Is this inexperienced teenager who has presented herself for interview *right* for her children? Can she trust her to keep them safe? If the answer is no, *then* what is she going to do? The first few times a working mother has to go through this, she has a very hard time believing it's happening. Here we are, living in a society that is obsessed with the welfare of children – a society that some people say even fetishises them – and this is how all the fine speeches translate into real life.

There you are, Deborah Eappen, opthalmologist. After twenty-plus years of education that cost someone hundreds of thousands of dollars, you can call yourself one of the lucky ones. You have a husband and a house and a job that allows you to work part-time while your children are small. Of course there will be penalties to pay for your defection: you will earn less, achieve less and so on. Even so, you have a lot more leeway than you might have done had you gone into law, business or another, more demanding branch of medicine. Still, you have to wonder. Why so many working women and dependent children, and why so little public interest in a system of childcare that is good for them? Why have employers and designers of professional career ladders not had to do *any* bending at all? Thus leaving women to scramble, and their children to suffer? From Deborah Eappen's point of view, the world is crazy.

2
The Cast of Characters

Where does that leave us?

The panics we have been looking at all touch on real problems – the absence of adequate supports for family life, the changes in the economy to which all families have had to adjust, the unravelling of the rules that once governed reproduction and marriage, the domestic consequences of maternal employment, and the effect all this shifting and unravelling has on children. The new conditions under which we live render traditional family values and strategies ineffective and so present a real moral challenge.

What to do? The best first step would be to look very carefully at the new conditions of family life, not just from the outside but also from the inside. The best next step would be to use this insider-outsider knowledge as a starting point for a discussion about how best to translate the old values and strategies into new ones that work.

In other words, what I am arguing for is a revolution – in

the way we define family life, in the way we define family policy – a revolution, finally, in the way we talk about and negotiate morality.

I know that this would be a vast undertaking. It would also, were it successful, undermine many of the hierarchies on which the worlds of work and politics are based. And so it is hardly surprising that right-wing thinkers and right-wing press barons would want to argue against it. This is not to say they ignore the problem. They are only too aware that the world they want to protect is sitting on domestic foundations that are no longer stable. Naturally, they want to do everything they can to stop the rot.

In their view, the best way forward would be to go backwards: return families to the old rules, the old hierarchies and the old ways of naming, shaming and punishing those who try to live outside them. They use family scandals as teaching points – proof that we have lost our way as a society, that the old ways were better. This steady diet of family panics does not, however, come out of thin air – they are about real people with real moral failings who really do illustrate our most urgent social contradictions. They tap into real anxieties about modern family life; but they all lead back to the same place.

The wrong people are having children, and the right people do not get proper support. In this back-to-front world, all our children are unsafe. That's the moral of every story: the scandals we've looked at so far have done much to hammer it home. We hear how the unmarried Mandy Allwood gets her babies free at Boots, while the married Diane Blood has to go through years of court cases, and finally go abroad for treatment, before she can have hers. The beleaguered Humphries family comes to stand for all families that are struggling to hold themselves together against the odds, and Deborah Eappen shows us what can happen when women 'abandon' their children for the selfish pleasures of the workplace.

What is the world coming to? This is the question underlying the stories we'll consider next. The focus now will be on the stock characters that the media use in order to explore the problems of modern family life. I'll begin with the Supermother, the Single Mother and the Selfless Mother; and then move on to the New Man, the Wicked Stepfather and the Paedophile. I'll look at the ways in which the panics about paedophiles affect public attitudes towards all men who are in charge of children.

None of these stock characters is anchored in reality. They all exist to give shape to our anxieties about female independence, and about men around children. They allow us to vent our fears concerning the rising divorce rate, and its consequences. They permit us to ask what effect all this might be having on children. Last but not least, they save us from the pain of thinking about them in any depth by proposing a simple explanation and a simple cure.

In the pages that follow, I shall be showing how these media projections do more than dominate just the popular debates about family life. They also define the terms of the more serious debates about mothers and fathers, paid and unpaid work, and the future of child-rearing. In so doing, they make it very difficult for even the most daring and innovative thinkers to ask the big questions.

The supermother

Meet Sue Roberts, high-flying 34-year-old executive at Scottish Power. She has a problem: her first child is due on 29 November. And there's this £4-billion take-over deal she's been trying to clinch by the end of that same month. The company in question is located in the US, which in the old days would have put her out of the loop as soon as her pregnancy had advanced to the point where she couldn't fly. But thanks to video links and conference calls, she's been able to remain at the centre of negotiations. She's been doing ten-hour days – and don't even ask about weekends.

She goes into the office on her due date, and it is business as usual. To quote the *Daily Mail*, the baby fails to 'arrive on schedule'. So the next morning, she is 'back again at her desk, making phone calls to the United States to try and put the seal on months of intense negotiations for the most important project she had ever been involved with'. And then, at possibly the most critical moment in the entire process, she goes into labour.

But this does not faze Sue Roberts – a woman, we are now told, who 'goes rock-climbing at weekends'. Despite the increasing pain of contractions, she spends a further three-and-a-half hours at her desk. 'Only my secretary knew what was happening,' she later said. It wasn't until 2 o'clock in the afternoon that she agreed to accompany her husband to the hospital. Speaking after the birth of her 7lb 5oz daughter, he claimed that his wife's dedication to her work did not surprise him: 'I would never have expected anything less from Sue . . . if she'd given up work any earlier, I would have been amazed.'

Her employers were equally 'supportive'. A spokesman for the company said that 'everyone in the company appreciates Sue's hard work and determination. She deserves double congratulations – both on the deal and . . . her beautiful baby daughter.' Their good grace becomes them. The deal she helped to broker made Scottish Power Scotland's biggest industrial firm and the seventh largest utility company in the world.[1] Presumably, she can write her own ticket from here on in. This may explain why she was brave enough to be photographed with her baby for a national newspaper that is not famous for championing working mothers. But in this case, the *Daily Mail* chose to go to the other extreme and portray Sue Roberts as the Amelia Earhart of the labour ward. The headlines were 'Businesswoman's Astonishing Timetable to Maternity: "I did 14 ten-hour days, worked 3½ hours into labour, clinched a £4 billion deal, and had a lovely baby!"'

When Sue Roberts looks back on that day, is she proud of her achievements or does she break out in a sweat at all the things that could have gone wrong? If labour had made her concentration go at a critical moment, and led her to make an error that botched the deal, would she have been able to forgive herself? If her daughter had been born premature, or weighing too little, would she have drawn a line between her long stressful hours and her baby's health? One thing is certain – *other* people would have.

In the public eye, there *is* no such thing as a good supermother. A good mother is, by definition, someone who shies away from super jobs that would get in the way of her children. As time goes on, Sue Roberts will have to work very hard to convince other people that her daughter is happy. At times, she will have to work just as hard at convincing herself. She'll need to defend herself against all those studies and features and leader articles which claim that children of working mothers do less well at school/make friends less easily/are more likely to suffer from depression. As time passes, she may find that any doubts which other people express about her choices, her child and her suitability as a mother are very hard to bear. But not as hard to bear as the doubts she keeps to herself as she shuffles between her two perfect masks.

Will she get to the point where she looks around her and thinks, why does anyone have to live like this? Why does being a high-ranking corporate type mean forgoing a personal life? Others have already done so, and publicly. This is how Brenda Barnes, $2-million-a-year head of Pepsi Cola's

North American division, explained her sudden decision to resign in September 1997: 'I am not leaving because my children need more of me; I'm leaving because I need more of them.' She will not have been surprised to find the press treating her departure with the exact same 'hysterical gloating' as it had the departures of Penny Hughes from Coca Cola UK in 1994 and Linda Kelsey from *She*, the magazine 'for women who juggle their lives'.[2] But she will also have known that, deep below the superficial stories that run in tabloids, there are many people out there who share her point of view, and many campaigns that are challenging the ethos and the work structures which forced her into her 'all or nothing' choice.

In the US there are so many people consulting and researching the 'work/life dilemma' that they are often referred to collectively as an 'industry'. In the UK we have New Ways to Work, Opportunity 2000, the Work/Life Forum, and the Daycare Trust, to name just a few, not to mention the campaign for paid parental leave and another to make employers more family-friendly, and the EOC campaign to get our equality legislation updated so that all parents can insist on family time without risking their jobs. Everyone working inside these organisations and campaigns sees the 'dilemma' as a work issue and a parents' issue, not a woman's issue. It's not women vs. the patriarchs, but men and women vs. an economic system that is squeezing them to breaking point.

Where to go from here? For Jane Buxton, author of *Ending the Mother Wars*, the answer is a 'workplace revolution'. She'd like to see companies restructure jobs so that women can give their children the care they deserve, while also doing their paid work to the highest professional standards. She does not think mothers and fathers are interchangeable, nor that they should have to pretend they are.[3] In *Having None of It*, Suzanne Franks suggests that women can achieve very little change on their own, given the direction of our economy and the continuing political marginalisation of any issue seen as belonging to women.[4] In *Madonna and Child: Towards a New Politics of Motherhood*, Melissa Benn is more hopeful, although she, too, stresses the importance of 'domestic democracy'. In her view, fathers need to change their lives to devote a 'meaningful half' of their lives to child rearing. But because all parents deserve more public support and better public services, she is adamant that there needs to be a political shift as well.[5]

In *Ask the Children: What America's Children Really Think of Working Parents*, Ellen Galinsky challenges the very terms of the work/life debate. For the past twenty years, she says, we've been arguing about whether or not mothers do their children harm by working. This debate excludes fathers and occludes the views of children. When she and her fellow researchers did consult the children of working parents, they discovered that working motherhood was not something most of them thought of as problematic in and of itself. What mattered to them was *how* their mothers worked, *and* how their fathers worked, how both their mothers and their fathers parented, and how they integrated their work and home responsibilities. While some arrangements failed or caused them sorrow or confusion, other arrangements seemed to be working. So how to tell the difference? The interviews Galinsky and her associates did with children led them to conclude that the conceptual tools parents used to describe their lives created more problems than they solved. To talk of 'balancing home and work' was to imply that the two halves were separate and somehow incompatible. To talk of 'juggling' was to imply that the moment you took your eyes off the balls, they all crashed to the floor. The term that she prefers, therefore, is navigating. The word navigating works, she says, 'because it is an ongoing process, not an ideal state . . . because it acknowledges the fluid interchanges among individual, work, family and community rather than treating them as separate spheres . . .' It's a word that reminds us that there are 'many forces and factors that combine to buffet or protect us . . . to stay our course and maintain an even keel, we need to be well attuned to the environment around us. *Navigating* works because we ultimately set the course we want to follow.'[6]

Her research indicated that family friendly policies at work alone were not enough to make 'navigation' possible. The most important thing was to equip parents so that they were in a position to try out new ways of integrating their home lives with their work lives. The radical implications of this practical sounding proposal become clearer if you look at projects such as the one led by Rhona Rapoport and Lotte Bailyn for the Ford Foundation in 1996.[7]

What they did in three major US corporations was to challenge the division between people's work and home lives in every office and every business, so that no one had to slink around to fit in normal domestic duties like children's doctors' visits and shopping trips for ailing aunts. Instead they arranged these things openly as and when they occurred, while they were arranging their work duties. This led to a dramatic increase in productivity. In spite of their success, it is very rare to see this kind of holistic approach put into practice.

In *The Time Bind*, the American sociologist Arlie Hochschild points out that the family-friendly policies offered by employers today fall into two distinct categories. There are the measures that help people get *to* work, and then there are those that help them get home. In her study of a prominent US corporation, she discovered that, surprise, surprise, the first variety were very popular while the second variety were under-subscribed. Even these were expendable; when the corporation suffered a downturn, the first thing to suffer was the Human Resources Department that had brought the family-friendly policies into being. Despite all the lip service this corporation paid to its family-friendly ethos, the work culture itself had not changed. If you wanted to stay ahead, if you wanted to keep the job you had and make sure your colleagues took you seriously, then you had to work long hours.

Arlie Hochschild is most famous for identifying the 'second shift' that most working women face when they drag themselves home at night. This is the shopping, the cooking, the ironing, the cleaning and the childcare that is still primarily their responsibility. In *The Time Bind*, she identifies a third shift, the psychological repair work that also falls to the woman in the family. This has always been part of a woman's workload; but when family time is compressed by the parents' work commitments, small emotional tensions have a way of turning into big tensions, misunderstandings multiply and important details get forgotten and overlooked. It will generally be up to the mother to 'make things right again', and that, she feels, is why many of the women she interviewed talked of being more relaxed at work.[8]

It was a controversial book, even though (or possibly because?) she was asking a very old question – the same question, in fact, that once spurred unions to campaign for the forty-hour week. How much time should any employer be allowed to take from its employees? Or to put it more broadly – can a society that does not give its citizens family time even call itself civilised?

It has become increasingly clear to those engaged in the work/life debate that the problems working mothers grapple with day in day out cannot be solved in a piecemeal way. They all derive from the way work and careers are structured, or rather from the assumption that all serious and able-bodied workers have wives to look after the domestic end of things. That assumption is central to our ideas not just about work but also about citizenship. At present there is no such thing as 'the right to give care'. As things stand now, a woman in a position like Sue Roberts' has no right to demand that her employers adjust to help her meet her domestic responsibilities. She must accept the perks on offer with good grace, or make her own compromises, or she must give up and leave.

If she does, she will of course be in a much stronger position than most of the other women she sees in her building – the part-time workers and dead-end-jobbers who must be content with their lot even though they don't earn what they deserve, because 'at least the job is easy to fit in with the children'. But in some ways, Sue Roberts and these other women have similar problems. What's more, she could possibly be in a position to help them one day. It is an article of faith in the work/life industry that a change of attitude must happen at the top before the people lower down the ladder can hope to see their working conditions improve.

The only way to spare working mothers their hard choices, say work/life campaigners, is to force all employers and economic planners to take the question of care seriously and factor it into everything they think and do. It's time, they say, that we understand how much we all depend on the carers of the world, and how we would come apart within days if they suddenly decided to withhold their services.

It is not always clear, however, if they themselves understand the implications of this statement. By making the shadowy domestic underpinnings of our economy visible, and by clamouring that domestic work should be better supported and better valued, they are in fact challenging the central ideas on which our economic system is based. But mostly they don't make this point. Mostly they confine themselves to the care problems suffered by people in paid employment. They tend not to see links between these problems and the difficulties facing full-time carers.

To understand why they lose sight of these links, we need

to look at all three of the stereotypes of modern motherhood. The supermother is not alone: she shares the stage with two other icons – the traditional stay-at-home mother and her presumed opposite, the single mother.

The stay-at-home mother

The press carries very few contemporary photographs of stay-at-home mothers. The fashion is to illustrate any discussion of this icon of propriety with photographs from the 1950s. The message these pictures give is that stay-at-home motherhood is a dying art that rampant feminism is fast destroying. There are exceptions: from time to time, a Sue Roberts type who is sick of working herself to death stages a spectacular change of heart. When she tells the papers that she's throwing it all up to go home to be with her children, she enjoys brief tabloid fame as a lone crusader against the ravages of feminism. But once she is home, we do not hear from her again.

When established stay-at-home mothers appear in the news, they are rarely there 'as themselves'. Instead they feature as props – the wife whose loving gaze reflects her husband back at twice his size, the mother whose tireless care is the key to her children's success. The message is that they have no identities of their own, and indeed do not wish to have identities of their own since happy husbands and thriving children are rewards in themselves. It's their job to do the caring, and this work is so all-consuming that there is no question of their leaving home to challenge the way the world defines their work, or to complain that the work they do is undervalued.

The image of traditional mothers is remarkably constant. No matter what we read into it, we all seem to see more or less the same thing. As a symbol, it has lost none of its power. For conservatives it stands for all that was good and beautiful about the way we were; for many married women and working mothers, it stands for everything they hope never to become. The only people who might be prepared to say this is an utter sham are the members of Full-Time Mothers.

Full-Time Mothers was founded in 1990, primarily to provide a support network for full-time mothers who felt passionate about their decision to stay with their children, wanted their work to be valued and were tired of being treated as oddballs or throwbacks. Politically, it's a broad church, and its members come from many different backgrounds. One woman I met at a meeting I attended in 1999 even had a 9-to-5 job. She was attending, she told me, because in her view there was no such thing as a part-time mother: 'We are all full-time.'

One of the first things Full-Time Mothers tells its new members is never to say, 'I'm just a mother'. It does not hold that all mothers should stay at home for ever, and it concedes that other members of a household or a family can also share in the care of children. But it is keen to support women who decide to remain home-based for longer than is now socially acceptable.

At present, the vast majority of stay-at-home mothers have children under five. Once children start school, the assumption is that a mother is 'free' to work. But what about the two-, three- or four-hour gap between the end of a normal school day and the end of a normal working day? What about half-terms and holidays, extra days, sports days, long or sudden illnesses? Full-Time Mothers gives women a chance to exchange their views on such matters: a necessary prerequisite to any decision, says its chairman, Jill Kirby, because 'there is never a simple answer to the question'.

Except, perhaps, the question of single mothers. 'The

whole of society will not benefit,' says Jill, 'if we force a mother to leave her child for a £5 an hour job that no one else wants.' She goes on to point out that it's not just single mothers who need to be worried about the new policies affecting them. There's a larger issue here that has to do with reproductive choice. If mothers lose the choice to stay at home when they decide their children need them there – if the only choice open to them is to leave their children and go out to work – then they can't really be said to have any choice at all.

This is why Full-Time Mothers sees itself as campaigning not just for its own constituency but for all mothers. It wants all women to have 'real choices'. It wants women who choose to stay at home with their children, whether it be for a year or a lifetime, to be properly supported. And it wants their work to be properly valued, both when they are at home and later on, if they return to work. It is not just insulting, but wrong, says Jill Kirby, to refer to full-time mothering as 'leisure' or a 'gap in employment'.[9]

In positioning itself like this, Full-Time Mothers is consistent with a massive international campaign to revalue unpaid domestic work. The ideas behind the campaign featured briefly in the news more than thirty years ago when Selma James founded Wages for Housework. Since then, she has had only a tiny amount of press coverage, little of it favourable. But no one could accuse her and related campaigners of aiming too low. The main target has been the system of National Accounts by which the United Nations calculates the relative wealth of all the countries in the world. These calculations go on to determine what gets funded and what does not, which kinds of workers are addressed in economic and social policy, and which are treated as if they didn't even exist. Until two years ago, anyone who reared her own children, did domestic work or produced her own food in this country didn't count: her work doesn't count as work.[10]

Thanks to the campaign to have women's work acknowledged, most countries keep track of the amount of unpaid
work in what they call a 'satellite account'. This, campaigners
are hoping, will change the way governments allocate their
resources and plan their economies. For unpaid domestic
workers to be on the political map, what they do must be
visible.

And now that women's unpaid jobs are better reflected in
the records, other care activists in the EU and the UN are
campaigning to get the work mothers traditionally do outside
the home, in schools and communities, counted in the political process. Some writers call this work 'small democracy'.
The British political philosopher Ruth Lister terms it 'informal politics' and claims that it is often overlooked because it
doesn't 'look' organised to traditionally organised politicians.
It tends to be less hierarchical and formulaic, and more par-
ticipatory. It's also more concerned with the kinds of domestic
and childcare issues that a traditional politician might see as
existing outside the realm of politics. In other words – it
looks a lot like Full-Time Mothers.

Put the Full-Time Mothers agenda next to the work/life
agenda, and it is immediately apparent that they are two sides
of the same coin. At the centre of both is a vision of an adult
who is able to make responsible free choices. This adult
recognises that over the course of a lifetime, all human beings
go through stages when they are entirely dependent on those
who care for them. At other stages, the tables turn and these
same human beings must take care of others. 'Taking care' of
others does not just mean staying at home with the children;
it can also mean earning the money for their support. If you
take the standpoint of a responsible adult who is trying to
come up with a plan that will keep a family of children
housed, fed and nurtured for the next twenty years, it is clear
that the strategy must be flexible, so that this adult can

change the ratio of paid to unpaid work as the family's needs change. For this to happen, the adult needs to be living in a society that takes people who give precedence to their unpaid work as seriously as those who give precedence to their paid work.

At present, we do not take unpaid workers as seriously as paid workers. In some very significant ways, we take them even *less* seriously now than we did in the bad old days of rampant patriarchy. Consider, for example, the support system which a traditional mother could count on in previous generations. She might not have figured as herself on the economic map, but she did figure as a dependant of a traditional breadwinner, who depended in turn on a steady job that gave him a family wage. Now we live in a time when there is no family wage, and no such thing as job security. Few families can make ends meet if just one adult is working, and few can make long-term plans – buy a house, for example – without taking a huge financial gamble. The high divorce rate means that it is foolhardy even to assume that your spouse will always be there for you. A stay-at-home mother who is not ready and qualified to jump back into the workforce at a moment's notice is a woman who may not be able to keep her family above the poverty line.

Even if she is lucky enough to have a steady husband with a steady job that brings in above-average earnings, her family will suffer financially. The gap between single and dual earner families is widening, and our taxation system gives the latter the advantage. We have a government that is deeply committed to the idea that all able-bodied adults should be in paid employment. The corollary of this is that stay-at-home motherhood is an unnecessary luxury.

But even as they urge all stay-at-homes to leave home, the government has stepped up the pressure on all parents – stay-at-homes included – to do a higher quality job. It's investing in a massive new programme of parent education to train us all to a higher standard – but when, exactly, is this better caring supposed to happen? During the lunch break?

The only way to confront this double message is to force the government to understand that caring work does not happen unless people have the time to do it. But that is not the only factor: it must also ensure that people who devote large chunks of their lives to care receive proper social supports. At present, they do not. Take our system of pension provision as an example. As a rule, pensions are designed for married men who stay in full employment for 45 years. They do not suit women who go in and out of employment because of their children. (Or indeed men who go in and out of employment because of the instability of our economy.) As work itself changes in response to global pressures, the old forms of social insurance are failing to protect women who are in part-time, casual or atypical jobs. The women who are most likely to be in these jobs are, of course, those whose employment is shaped and constrained by family commitments.

All this ought to be evident to most people in their everyday lives. Most people know women who are struggling financially because the supports a mother could depend on ten, twenty years ago just aren't there any more. And most of the stay-at-home mothers which we know in our own lives bear no resemblance whatsoever to the housewife icon in our morning papers. But still people believe this icon. And so it is that the prejudices against stay-at-home mothers are never properly challenged, the political campaigns on their behalf never quite get off the ground, and the link between their needs and those of working mothers remain elusive.

The single mother

There is one very brief and telling exception – the revolt against the government in 1997, when it tried to cut benefits to lone-parent families. The nation was outraged that these parents, who were so needed at home, were going to be forced out into work. Even the tabloids were livid – including those which had worked so hard, and for so many years, to mass market the image of the single mother as an overgrown council estate teenager who was content to put her feet up on the table while her undisciplined children ran riot around her; who never took the fag out of her mouth except to bleat an expletive; who had got pregnant in the first place because she wanted to jump the housing queue, because her life was empty, because she had learned nothing at school, because she wanted someone to love, because her children's many feckless fathers just wouldn't buckle down.

Now suddenly, the single mother was none of these things. Instead, she became the 'Latest Casualty of Rampant Feminism' – a woman who fervently believed that her most important work was at home, and who was now being hounded into work against her will. But it was not only tabloids who were upset about this. Harriet Harman, the minister responsible, also received the hammering of her career in the qualities, in a heated exchange on the 'Today' programme, and even from her fellow Labour MPs. How could she, the author of a book that promoted caring for young children as a valuable occupation, support such a policy? Audrey Wise, MP for Preston, expressed extreme concern about 'an attitude that says all parents of small children should be willing to go to work cleaning or shelf filling and leaving their children with somebody else'. Children would suffer from the cuts, she said. Frances Cook, MP for Stockton North, called the cuts 'primitive, unjustified, and totally unwarranted', while Alice Mahon, the MP for Halifax, termed them 'punitive and cruel'. She could not understand how Harman could support cuts she had 'opposed so eloquently' the year before. If the new deal proposals became compulsory, as so many Labour MPs now feared they would, 'it would be a piece of social engineering that Stalin would be proud of'. She then added, 'What it is saying is that if you are a widow or a battered wife, or if you are a mother left literally holding the baby, then you will not have the choice to look after your children. If women want to go back to work, that is fine, but women have to be given the choice.' Labour had won the general election, she said, by promising that 'things could only get better'. She could only conclude that it 'had missed the verse on lone parents'.[11]

But so, I would argue, has everyone else. Like the super-mother and stay-at-home mother labels, the lone parent/ single mother label is extremely misleading. Even the defenders of single mothers use the term as if it implied youth, low educational levels and a fair degree of poverty. And it is rare for them to challenge the prevailing view that single motherhood is an unstoppable trend.

On first inspection, the statistics would seem to indicate just that. The total number of single lone mothers has increased fivefold in twenty years. In 1992, there were 490,000 single lone mothers in Britain with responsibility for over half a million children. But that is out of a total of 1,400,000 lone parent families. There are (people tend to forget this when they glide over the statistics too quickly) many other types of lone-parent families. A small percentage (8.6 per cent) are headed by men, and 4.3 per cent by widows. About one in four is headed by separated mothers, and just under a third by divorced mothers. Many of these single mothers are (yes, it's shocking, but isn't it obvious?) also stay-at-home mothers.

Although the average age of a single lone mother is 25, the term covers both teenagers whose conceptions were unplanned and older women who deliberately set out to start a family alone. It's not a static state, either: the average length of time a person will spend as a lone parent is four years.[12]

Even if you separate out the teenage mothers, the trends are not quite as worried moralists would have us believe. There was indeed a rise in teenagers giving birth out of wedlock during the 1980s, especially amongst women from poorer backgrounds: this was in sharp contrast to marked reduction in teenage fertility elsewhere in Europe. But if you combine the numbers of teenagers giving birth inside and outside marriage, it emerges that there were 10,000 fewer teenage maternities in 1991 than in 1981, and 42,000 fewer than in 1971. In 1971 there were 67.3 maternities per 1,000 teenage women. In 1992 there were only 40.4 maternities per 1,000 teenage women.[13]

The most significant shift in the past three decades may not be a rise in the number of women actively choosing to have children on their own, but a decline in the shotgun marriage. In the early 1970s, an unplanned pregnancy often resulted in the couple marrying before the arrival of the baby. Now that there is not the same sort of pressure to get married, it is far more likely that the couple will not marry but cohabit. Like shotgun marriages, these relationships are not particularly stable. But when a shotgun marriage couple splits up, the mother gets counted as separated or divorced. If a woman has lived with the father of her child without first getting married, she will be counted as a single lone parent. 'One consequence of the decline of the shotgun marriage may, therefore, have been to effect a net shift of women from one lone parent category to another.'[14]

The story of single fathers is equally complex, and different for different classes and age groups. It is even harder to understand them as a group than to understand single mothers as a group, because fathers who do not reside with their children suffer from statistical invisibility: except in the form of that other media icon – Disaffected Youth. But even if you take the group that comes closest to this description – those young inner city men who are failing to walk into steady jobs and marriages in the way their parents might have done twenty and thirty years ago – the story remains ambiguous. Young fathers, like young mothers, are more likely to be socially and economically disadvantaged, and with few educational qualifications. They are more likely to be unemployed than men of the same age who don't have children. They're less likely to maintain contact with their children than divorced or separated fathers.

But a recent study of young, lone inner-city fathers in Newcastle found their subjects expressing a far greater interest in fathering than these statistics might suggest. It was not designed to be a representative study; only 2 of the 40 men interviewed had no contact at all with their children. The idea was to define this unusually committed group's views and experiences of fatherhood. It found that their attitudes about the unimportance of marriage and the normality of lone-parent families did help to shape their choices. But it was also clear that the policies, agencies and economic realities that framed their lives and opportunities made it very hard for them to pull everything together into something resembling an independent settled life. 'For example, to commit to a job may mean moving away from their neighbourhood and losing vital family support. To commit to more involvement in fatherhood may mean not being able to accept a home in another part of the city. Therefore the degree to which young single men can be involved as fathers is likely to fluctuate according to a range of influences beyond their control as they balance time, housing, finance and other issues.'[15]

None of these research findings is particularly surprising if you approach the question of fatherhood from the father's point of view. Step into his shoes and the problems he has to solve – about work, care, housing, money, long-term security – are the same problems married and cohabiting fathers have to face; they have a lot in common, too, with the problems facing full-time mothers and working mothers who work full- and part-time. But public discussions of mothers and fathers hardly ever take the point of view of mothers and fathers. They keep to the tradition of looking at them from the outside, through the wrong end of the telescope. They divide to rule by using labels that make a nonsense of real life, and it's this, more than anything else, that makes the way we really live so hard to understand.

New men

The standard line in the work/life world is that young men are becoming more militant about their right to a home life, and that even more would do so if they thought they could. But to change the culture, as these campaigners are always saying, you need the men at the top to lead by example. Their own culture is full of stories about CEOs daring to tell their underlings of their desire to spend more time with their children, wives and mothers, about Australian he-men who are reluctant to admit to their desire to spend more time at home, but who then allow their masks to fall after doing group work with their supervisors and finding out it's all right for men to feel that way. And then there are the men who try and fail to get their employers to adjust their schedules, and who then have to take them to court.

Not long before Brenda Barnes left Pepsi Cola, a former EMI executive won damages of £9,020 for constructive dismissal over the way the company suddenly increased the amount of time he was expected to spend travelling from 40 per cent (as stipulated in his contract) to 75 per cent of his work year. Most of the travelling was abroad – to Tokyo and San Francisco and all over Europe. EMI presented the sudden increase, says James Whyte, as a 'fait accompli'. The company had even wanted him to go to San Francisco on the day his wife was expecting their first daughter. He had refused them 'out of frustration and anger' and quit.

'It was an enormous issue for me. Why would I be willing to accept the 75 per cent requirement? I had a young family. There had been no notice for me to raise my objections. I was required to start in New York in a week and a half's time . . . I was a little guy up against an enormous company.' He risked a lot by walking out, he said after the case. He had been unemployed, his wife had had to go out to work, he'd lost his car and his health insurance and many other perks. 'But if I didn't do it, I would never have seen my daughter starting to crawl, walk and recognise me as daddy. It is part of common sense and human decency. Seeing your children grow up only happens once. People aren't scared to put their family first any more.'

But it takes more than courage to put things right. Because, you see, James Whyte did not win his case because the court found his employers guilty of sex discrimination. He won it because of breach of contract.[16] As it stands now, the sexual discrimination law does not protect men who are discriminated against because they want to be active fathers. But there is much pressure for the law to be changed, and certainly we have never had a government quite as keen on getting more fathers to spend more time with their children, and especially their sons.

One of its most media-friendly efforts is the national 'Dads and Lads' literacy campaign to encourage fathers to read to their sons in offices, factories and even prisons. The hope is that this will rid reading of its 'effeminate' image and thus provide boys with more positive literate role models. Lots of famous men have lent their names to the campaign and have gone public with lists of their favourite books from childhood. Success at the 'hard end of the business' is somewhat hampered by the fact that Jack Straw has continued the Tory policy of cutting the funding of the prison education services. There has also been resistance from prison authorities to the idea of equipping visiting rooms with books for fathers to read to their children. But charities like Kids VIP have managed to overcome this obstacle in some prisons. One of these is Wellington prison, where Martyn Clark was nearing the end of an 18-month sentence for burglary when the *Observer* photographed him reading his son a book called *The Great Flood*. Martyn has two children by his fiancé; one is a baby, and the other is a toddler. And when they come to visit, the two-year-old 'gets bored and starts running around', Martyn told the reporter. 'He needs something to keep his mind occupied.' Reading him picture books had proved to be the perfect solution. Not only had it allowed father and son to get closer, it had also changed Martyn's own attitude to education. 'I missed my opportunities and I don't want that for Jason.'

The educational service at Wellington prison was hoping to capitalise on such changes of heart by introducing 'family learning days'. 'The men come to us to deal with their own literacy problems so that they can help their own children,' explained Jean Bridgman, head of the educational service. 'That can be a big motivator. There is no doubt that if you want to fix these problems, you have to fix the family.'[17] By fixing the family, or so this line of thinking goes, you can break the cycle of under-achievement that might otherwise condemn little boys like Jason to follow their fathers into a life of crime.

Unlike so many other recent initiatives to break the cycle of under-achievement, this is one which gives the father a positive aim, a message that he is the one with the power to make or break his child's future, and a clear understanding of what he needs to do. But the aims of the fathering movement are far more ambitious than this humble example might suggest. As Claire Rayner said when the RSA launched its campaign for paid paternity leave in 1996, a 'society made up of adults who share parental skills and concern would rear a much more balanced and contented generation of children. The future would be a much more helpful one if mothers were joined by fathers in caring for children as well as bearing them. And they could turn the macho culture on its ears. We're halfway there anyway; when I was a midwife in the fifties, the presence of a father in the labour ward was unheard of. Now, men who stay out are in a minority and considered wimps. In a paternity leave-fuelled future, men who couldn't take care of their children would be seen as worse than wimps.'[18]

Change will be slow, Adrienne Burgess predicts in her defence of modern paternity, *Fatherhood Reclaimed*. 'Many of the economic and social functions that are beginning to force men to re-evaluate their functions are, as yet, in their infancy. There is also no point in simply dumping fathers on their children and children on their fathers. Skill acquisition has to be part of it, and network support, and these do not develop overnight . . . The images of fatherhood with which we are surrounded would have to be challenged and broadened, and the reality of fathers' private lives made more visible.'[19]

This is already happening. Take as an example Tony Madrugo, self-employed wholesaler, who has two children aged 10 and 13 by a woman with whom he lived for six years. The split was 'not too acrimonious' but it was heart-breaking. His relationship with his children he described as 'great' and he had always paid for their upkeep. He only discovered he had no rights when he went to a solicitor after his ex-partner changed the children's last names. 'I felt devastated. I had lived with these children. I was a good father. I paid for them and yet I had no power to look after them. I felt used – just a money machine.' He went to court and although he had to represent himself, he won on appeal. 'It was an enormous relief. It was a long battle and I shouldn't have had to have it in the first place. Now I feel I have a voice again. I ring the school and they are now happy to fax me my children's progress or discuss any problems they are having. To me it means I can be a proper father.'[20]

And gradually, the law is moving in his favour. In July 1998, Lord Irvine extended parental rights to all unmarried new fathers – now numbering 180,000 a year – who put their names on their children's birth certificates.[21] In September of the same year, a judge in Wiltshire awarded custody to a father not because he had proved his wife deficient but because she worked full-time and he did not.[22] Last November, Mr Justice Cazalt, a judge in the High Court Family Division, ruled that a two-year-old boy should remain with his father and used the occasion to say that, 'Fathers are much better equipped to look after their children nowadays than they were some ten years ago.' The percentage of children going to fathers has doubled in the past year, but from only one per cent to only two per cent. Generally speaking, it only happens when the mother is a drug addict, has a depressive illness, or suffers from a health or social problem of comparable gravity.[23]

Children still stay with their mothers in 95 per cent of cases. Even so, the tiny swing in favour of fathers has caused anxiety amongst working women who earn more and/or work longer hours than their children's fathers. The fear is that judges could come to appreciate active fathers without overcoming their traditional prejudices against working

mothers, and the result could be women losing their only
remaining set of traditional privileges.

This anxiety goes some way to explaining the sporadic
explosions of hostility by working-mother journalists against
self-promoting 'new fathers'. But there is deeper and better
organised resistance to the idea, too. The think-tank world is
awash with pamphlets arguing that new fathering is all
wrong, and not what most men need or want. Not all go as far
as the American author Francis Fukuyama, who would like to
see women returning to dependency and men stepping back
into responsible authority. David Popenoe, another key figure
in the US debate, advocates what he calls a 'modified' traditional script, with women returning to home-based roles only
during the very earliest years of child-rearing.[24]

Author and journalist Melanie Phillips suggests something
much along the same lines. She is particularly concerned
about what she calls the Sex-Change State, or rather the way
the state plays Daddy to single mothers, thus making low-
income fathers superfluous. She does not advocate an abrupt
return to 'the way it was'. In her utopia, as in Popenoe's, some
women work some of the time, but they return home when
they are rearing young children. It is not important, she says,
for fathers to stick around at this point: they exercise a far
better influence on their children if they are absent. Children
do not need nurturing from their fathers, she believes. What
they need more is a father to serve as a symbol. He is 'the
other parent who made me', and the one who can be counted
on to pay the bills.[25]

If he has a job, that is. Opponents of the breadwinner
revivalists are forever pointing out that the key issue here is
poverty. The Fukuyamas, Popenoes and Phillipses of the world
do not agree. Poverty, they say, is not the cause of family breakdown. It's family breakdown that is the cause of poverty.
Discussions about fathering – like those about mothering – are

never just about what goes on in our homes. They're about political ideology and economics, and so doomed never to be resolved. But the public views on proper paternal behaviour are changing nonetheless.

This change is most evident in extreme cases like the Michael Stone trial in 1998. There were no cheap remarks when Shaun Russell, father of Josie, wept openly in front of the cameras at the news that Stone had been convicted of killing his wife and his older daughter, and leaving Josie for dead. The evidence on which Stone was convicted has since been questioned – it is possible that he was 'fitted up' by the man who tied him most closely to the crime, and by a second witness as well. But the visual evidence in the papers tells another story. In one corner there is Michael Stone, the heroin addict with a history of violence and a severe and untreatable anti-social disorder. He has a midnight shadow and a burning cigarette, and he's staring straight into the camera with those strange, deranged eyes. And then, right next to him, is the smiling, unsuspecting Russell family on a picnic blanket.

This is the picture Stone destroyed. Shaun Russell will be spending the rest of his life picking up the pieces. And so no one would have dreamed of faulting him for deciding after that tragedy to give up his symbolic breadwinner role as academic and return with his surviving daughter to the Welsh hills where she had spent most of her young life. It was understood that he would be central to Josie's life and was indeed beyond reproach as a nurturing father. Everything he said to the press supported that impression. If he had been making the same statement as an unmarried or separating father – in other words, as an instigator of family breakdown – he would have raised eyebrows and prompted derision. But because it was clear beyond the tiniest shadow of a doubt that he had not brought this tragedy on himself, the public and the press were 100 per cent on his side when he spoke of his whole way of life changing on discovery that Josie was 'still alive and needing help'.

He spoke openly about his feelings – his elation at the news of the verdict, which had been followed by feelings of sadness; his inability to hate Stone, who had psychological problems; his sympathy for Stone's mother and sister; his anger at his loss; the terrible images he still had of his wife and older daughter in the mortuary; his gratitude for Josie, whose brightness and courage kept him on track; and his fears for her safety now that she wanted to walk by herself to her new school. He talked of how she was struggling with her work there; she would always be speech-impaired, but with the right sort of help she could even go to university. 'My job is important,' he told the press. 'But not as important as getting Josie stable emotionally, psychologically, with some degree of attainment.'[26]

Like Whyte and Madrugo, he's not afraid to speak openly about this – his other, more important job. And when he does, everyone knows that even if he approaches this job with courage, ingenuity, stamina, humility and humour, he will not be able to do it unless he also has the right sort of environment for Josie and a huge amount of outside support. If the fathering movement gets its way, it will be possible for men to speak in these terms and be heard without first having to lose half their family to a murderer. But there is one rather large problem standing in the way of fathers getting more contact with their children across the board. Despite an increased acceptance that some men are capable of being good nurturers, there is next to no confidence that *all* men can be trusted to be left alone with them. The problem, one might say, is how to distinguish between the Shaun Russells of this world and the Michael Stones.

Natural born stepfathers

For every good father who finds his way into the papers, there must be twenty ersatz ones who make your blood run cold. Take Paul Gaye, the heroin addict who was convicted in April 1998 of killing Suzanne Rarity, his girlfriend's seven-year-old daughter. He had moved in with Angela, the mother, in April 1997, from which time he had 'dominated family life'. The mother told the jury that she had not been allowed to get near her daughter. 'Do you think if I could have done something to save her, I wouldn't have done it?' On 16 June, Gaye decided that Suzanne was lying when she said she had washed her hands. He locked her in her room and kept the keys, and that was that. During the week that followed, the last week of her life, she did not leave the house once. As Charles Garside, prosecuting QC, put it, 'Essentially Gaye took charge of her.' During this time he inflicted a hundred injuries on the girl. He punched her, beat her with a stick, attacked her with a table fork and pulled out her hair with a laundry brush. On 22 April, she died after five heavy blows that caused internal bleeding. Police found her curled up on a mattress on the floor in her bedroom – but not for another 36 hours, because as soon as Gaye saw he had beaten the girl to death, he ran away. He left the keys to her room on the mantelpiece, along with a letter to Angela explaining that he was 'scared of what people might think of me . . . It was all down to me. I'm so confused at the moment. I just wish it was me dead and not her.'[27]

This could pass for remorse. But what to make of John Sherrington, who 'punched the air in triumph' when his murder charge was dropped at the Old Bailey in November 1997? It was not clear if he had killed his girlfriend's 18-month-old baby single-handed, or if he had killed the baby jointly with her, or if he had just stood by doing nothing while the mother did it. Prosecutors in 'joint enterprise' cases need to prove who struck the fatal blow. Because no one could prove who had done so, in the end John Sherrington and the baby's mother, Lavinia Adams, had to be tried on lesser charges.

But as one police officer said, 'When you know the sort of things they did to her, this is a travesty.' These things included blows that caused her skull fractures, and haemorrhaging of the brain. A tape that John Sherrington made of his version of childcare has him telling the toddler: 'I've got a mixture for you. You can have some car wash mixed with bleach, mixed with paint. A really nice drink for you. You'll love it.' Later on he tells Lavinia, 'I'll get her in a lock'. This meant getting her in a judo lock between his legs. Apparently he had done this on a number of occasions. The tape records the child screaming, and John Sherrington taunting her, saying 'Got you in a lock there, look at her.' Then he tells the baby he won't mark her as she has a hospital appointment that same week. At this point, Lavinia makes a weak effort to intervene, while 'making a note to herself to buy bubble bath and talking about wanting to do the washing up'.[28]

In the case of Lauren Creed, five-year-old victim of yet another violent stepfather, it was a neighbour who made a tape of a conversation in which Lauren admitted to being routinely beaten. 'Dad punched me in the belly today. Slapped me. Punched me.' The neighbour took the tape to the police, but somehow nothing got done about it. When she was found dead, she had 167 fresh bruises and abrasions on her body and a fractured rib. Her liver had been crushed. According to pathologists, this happened either as a result of the man kicking or punching her as she stood against the wall, or by stamping on her as she lay on the floor. Lauren's mother, a senior RAF aircraftwoman based at Cottishall, Norfolk, had – like Lavinia Adams and Angela Rarity – apparently failed to lift a finger in her daughter's defence. The news reports all suggest the same explanation for this terrible failure. They were 'obsessed' with their boyfriends, and cared about them more than they cared about their children's safety. There were other parallels: Lauren's stepfather, Graham Sate, had a serious drug problem, just like Paul Gaye. With a history of violence, he was only ten months out of prison when he killed Lauren. He had previously been convicted of attempted murder and of an attack on a fellow prison inmate.

He had known the mother, Sharon, before she was a mother. He had a grievance against Lauren because she was the result of a short relationship the mother had with someone else. Like Gaye and Sherrington, he was a stepfather-by-default.[29] So, incidentally, was the man who administered a brutal caning to the boy who put into question a British parent's right to smack, by winning £10,000 damages at the European Court of Human Rights in 1998 for 'inhuman and degrading punishment'. It was the boy's natural father who helped him to bring the suit.[30]

The General Household Survey of 1991 showed that 8 per cent of all families with dependent children contained at least one stepchild. There were half a million step-families, with just over three-quarters of a million dependent children in all, and just over a quarter of a million 'new' children born of the new partners. This was not counting the large number of children who visited other step-families on holidays and weekends. If current trends continue, then one in every eight children can expect to spend part of his or her childhood living in a step-family. It is hard to understand which kinds of problems are specific to such families because different surveys and statistics define the term differently, and few distinguish between the myriad family forms that fall into the category. Neither do they pay enough attention to the complex links between step-family households and other households.[31]

To use my own case as an example – my two stepchildren have always resided with their mother, and my two older children from my first marriage spent most of their childhood living with me. But my stepchildren spent a lot of time with me too, and my children spent a lot of time with their father. And the arrangements have changed many, many times over the past ten years. This means that any researcher trying to come to grips with the problems in my household would have to look at the two other households with which it has been so closely linked, and also examine the erratic quality of cooperation between our household and the others, not to mention the changing relationships between the two sets of stepchildren, and between all four stepchildren and the two 'new' children to whom they are all related!

Most research on step-families does not look at this jungle of variables, and so can present only a partial picture of what is going on in them. But even if you bear all these caveats in mind, the partial research on these families still makes for disturbing reading. A recent Scottish study found that children in step-families were more likely to leave home at 16 or 17. Another study that looked at homeless young people from 'disrupted' families suggested that such families were far less tolerant of wayward adolescent behaviour: 'There has been a rise in the number of reconstituted families, and it would be wrong to assume that reconstituted households continue to have the same commitment to long-term support of young people living within the household.' If research showed that more children from step-families left home early, it was 'not simply because of conflict with step-parents; some birth parents want the young person to leave so that they can get on with their new life. The family script alters and young people feel excluded.'[32]

In a cross-cultural study drawing upon statistics from Canada, the US, Britain and Australia, psychologists Martin

Daly and Margo Wilson found that step-parents are massively over-represented as child batterers and sexual abusers. Even when you correct for variables like poverty and maternal age, the imbalance is still there. And a child living with a step-parent is 100 times more likely to suffer 'lethal battering' than is a child living with its natural parents. The statistics show that natural parents can be killers too. But as a rule, they use less violent means, and often they kill their children by including them in a 'successful suicide'.

Daly and Wilson have also studied the treatment accorded to 'step' offspring in other mammals. Because they have found similar patterns, they posit that the problem has a genetic basis. They do concede that social factors might exist, too: adopted children are not natural offspring, either, but they do not run the same risks as stepchildren.[33]

Adoptive parents are screened and vetted and overseen by authorities. Procedures in different countries are not the same, but as a rule people do not adopt children casually. It has to be something they want to do. To get through the formalities, they also have to be pretty organised and determined. But the routes to step-parenthood are very different. There may be people who decide to fall in love with a parent after first forming an attachment with his or her children, but as a rule it's the other way around. First you fall in love with the adult and then, when you set up house with this person, you agree to take on the children.

It's a position that is riddled with difficulties. If the children are very, very young when you take them on, you might just be able to forge a 'real' relationship with them. But even if you are replacing a parent who has died, older children tend to resent any effort on your part to assume parental authority. If you and your partner have differing ideas about child-rearing, you can expect him or her to undermine you too, which means you have even less to go on when trying to create a positive relationship with them. If the children's other parent resents your presence, he or she can also do a lot to turn the children against you. If that other parent tells them you have 'no right' to tell them what to do, he/she is merely stating the facts. Because as a step-parent, you have no legal rights: as far as the law is concerned, you hardly exist.

If you have experience with children, you can sometimes find a way around these obstacles – with time. According to the National Stepfamily Association, it takes between 2 and 10 years for the relationship to settle. If you are a woman who has often had to make the best of situations in which you do not have as much power as you might like, you might be able to make the best of this one too. You will not, in any event, feel less of a 'woman' because of it. For a man who associates dominance with masculinity, the constraints of step-parenthood are likely to be more problematic, however.

There are seven stepfathers for every stepmother. Many have little or no experience of children, and nowhere to go for information or support. Given the circumstances under which most of them operate, it is a miracle that anyone at all ends up making a success of it. Given the disturbing statistics, and the way they seem to confirm our folklore about wicked step-parents, it is not surprising that step-parents suffer from stigma. But even though many stepfathers complain that they are too often considered guilty until proven innocent,[34] few would argue that the prejudice stems *just* from the fact that they are step-parents. The main count against them is that they are men: men taking care of other men's children.

The paedophile

'In the middle of the night, Miss Clavel woke up and said, "Something is not right!" And afraid of a disaster, Miss Clavel ran fast and faster . . .' These lines come from *Madeline*, the children's book about a little girl in a French boarding-school who is rushed to the hospital in the middle of the night with appendicitis. They've come back to me often over the past ten years, most notably during the Cleveland abuse scare in the late 1980s and the satanic abuse swoops that followed in the Orkneys and elsewhere. What actually happened in these cases I am not qualified to say, but the pattern of the coverage is there for anyone to see. The stories begin under cover of darkness. The rescue operations are based not on a solid bed of facts but on hunches. There's a sense of urgency, a conviction that when it comes to children it is always better to be safe than sorry. A fear of what might be going on behind closed doors, that turns into a panic as well-meaning child protection officers run fast and faster . . .

And the more they look, the more they find. In the decade since the Cleveland scandal, there has been an explosion in abuse cases involving children in the care of men who are not their fathers. Priests, ministers, scout leaders, teachers and children's home workers have been exposed as child abusers. The NSPCC goes so far as to claim that a million children are 'sexually, physically, or emotionally abused' each year.[35] As the epidemic grows, so too does the definition of abuse. It is now a term that lumps together very serious incidents and types of emotional abuse which many might think were just part of growing up. (An example would be the new term 'sibling attack', which people used to refer to as 'children squabbling in the back of the car'.) Now and again, a lone voice expresses concern about the dangers of conflating all forms of abuse: in exaggerating the significance of minor and more commonplace incidents, these critics say, they diminish the importance of rarer, serious cases in which there is real and lasting damage.[36] But these warnings have had little effect on the public imagination as

regards their feelings about men with responsibility for children.

Each new abuse case confirms the fear that there are other
child abusers who are not getting caught because their victims are too scared to speak. The difficulties of disclosure are
well rehearsed. It's generally agreed, also, that disclosure
needs to be made easier. To this end, there has been a massive
increase in help lines and other forms of outreach. Police
investigating long-ago abuse in children's homes routinely do
mass mailings to former residents, soliciting information
about former home workers and at the same time reminding
them that they could receive compensation under the criminal injuries compensation scheme – up to £17,500 – if they
help to secure a conviction.[37]

These scandals that reach far into the past feed on the mys-
tique of the crime's invisibility: just as you never know how
much abuse is going on, so it is impossible to identify an
abuser because he probably looks as normal as you or me. At
the same time, we've managed to build up a composite picture of this archetypal villain. Like Sidney Cooke and Robert
Oliver, he carries outward signs of evil that are clearly visible.
There's something 'blank' about him, an absence of remorse,
that sets him apart from other people.[38] He is not quite
human and can be treated accordingly. When mobs went after
Robert Oliver in the autumn of 1997, and when they forced
Sidney Cooke to take refuge in a series of West Country
police stations the following spring, some commentators
expressed concern about the level of public hysteria, and
about the way the tabloid press was trying to raise the tem-
perature even higher with headlines like, 'BEWARE THIS EVIL
PERVERT', 'SEX KILLER TOLD: YOU ARE NOT WANTED HERE', and
'CHILD SEX KILLER: HE'S JUST SICK AND PATHETIC'.[39]

In the *Guardian*, Decca Aitkenhead wondered if the expressions of rage had anything to do with the fact that

'paedophiles are one of the few groups you can respectably hate'. And in *The Times*, William Rees Mogg put the blame on a 'dumbed-down, hyped-up' culture that was eroding the ancient British virtue of common sense: 'to some extent, the mothers who . . . demonstrated against the police are actually putting their children at risk, because they interfere with police arrangements to protect children in general.'[40]

There was indeed corroboration of this claim. During the Cooke panic, the probation service warned that the surveillance system its officers had developed to keep tabs on known paedophiles was 'close to breakdown' following that month's wave of vigilante attacks and media 'outings' of sex offenders. In one case, a man living in the same block of flats as a convicted child molester was severely beaten after a local paper outed his neighbour. In another, 400 people descended on a probation hostel, convinced that it housed convicted paedophiles, when in fact it did not. In a third case, a highly dangerous sex offender went underground after he was outed in the local press. In a fourth, another sex offender who had been under 24-hour-a-day surveillance, and who also disappeared after being outed, was only traced after he began offering babysitting services. But once he saw the game was up, he disappeared again. 'Offenders, once they are driven out of contact,' said Gill Mackenzie, chief probation officer of Gloucestershire, 'are likely to be a much greater risk.'[41]

'We've gone from one extreme to the other,' said Penny Buller, chief probation officer for East Sussex, during the Oliver panic. 'No interest in paedophiles, and now this.' It did little to solve the larger problem. Home Office research shows that most child molesters operate alone and sexually assault children they know.[42] A 1990 Scottish study of 89 families referred to the Dundee Royal Infirmary for problems connected with sexual abuse, found that the abuser was a stranger in only 3 per cent of cases. The number of children who are murdered by strangers in this country annually is tiny. In 1992 it was 2. In 1993 it was 8. In 1994 it was 4, in a population of nearly 12 million children. The national annual average over the past twenty years is just under seven. The figures for abduction are considerably higher. In 1992, for example, there were 54. But most of the abductors were not strangers but estranged parents.[43]

Although these figures do get trotted out in articles about child safety, they do not seem to stick. When the children's charity, Kidscape, did a survey of parental attitudes in 1993, it found that the number one worry for 95 per cent of the respondents was abduction by strangers.[44] The fear of abduction is one of the things that has led this generation of parents to supervise their children far more closely than they were supervised themselves. In Dr Gill Valentine's 1996 study of 'stranger danger', she found that 95 per cent of parents imposed restrictions on their children's play out of fears for their safety, and indeed felt under immense social pressure to keep to those new norms.[45] The change to these new norms has been swift; in 1971, 80 per cent of 7- and 8-year-olds in England travelled to school by themselves or with friends. By 1990, that figure was down to 10 per cent. In 1990, 23 per cent of parents described their children as 'outdoors children' – a sharp drop from 60 per cent in the early 70s.[46]

If the community couldn't accept the idea of people like Oliver in its midst, Penny Buller told the press, then perhaps it was time to change the way we sentenced them.[47] Perhaps the lynch mobs were trying to tell us, in their crude and primitive way: we don't want child molesters walking free in our midst; we want to keep them locked up for as long as possible; when they're freed we want them tagged and monitored and barred from any form of contact with children.

The more temperate general public assumes, of course, that they will have had a fair trial beforehand; that, barring the odd miscarriage of justice, it's only the guilty who will bear the brunt of these draconian measures. In fact, no one who is accused of these offences can be sure of a fair trial.

It used to be very difficult – next to impossible, some would say – to secure a conviction in cases involving child abuse. But now it is perhaps too easy. The jury never gets the background information that might put a case into context. The motives of the children are rarely called into doubt because in the present climate it's considered 'legal suicide' to do so. Most important, this is the only crime for which there is no need for corroborative evidence. The system as it now stands also makes it very easy for children who have not been abused to 'get rid of' step-parents they do not like. And it does not guard against children being manipulated by parents seeking revenge against ex-partners who have wronged them. The fact that there's serious money to be gained from the exercise makes it all the more likely that the system will be abused.

You might like to think that there is rarely any smoke where there isn't fire, and that nice, reasonable, responsible, middle-class people need not worry about their motives being misconstrued by the law. But consider a 1997 'family bath' case brought by a natural father concerned about his children's stepfather's habit of walking around his house nude. He also objected to the mother and her new partner taking baths with the children. The first judge was appalled and ordered that the children be removed from their home and handed over to their father. The appeal judge, Lady Justice Butler Sloss, decided that the previous judge had overreacted when he decided to take the children away from their mother, but she did add that the stepfather had been unwise. 'In a happy, well-run family, how members behave in the privacy of their own home is their business, and no one else's. But where the family may be subject to public or private law, there is a danger that their activities, no matter how innocent or well-intended, can be misconstrued. A new partner, in my view, has to be careful with children who are not his own. New partners, particularly male partners, should be cautious in their approach to such issues as nudity when staying in the same household as their partner's children.'[48]

This is sensible advice, but it skirts the central question that no one in polite society wants to ask. *Can* all men be trusted with children? Even if they can be trusted with their own, does this mean they can be trusted with other people's children? Much as those of us promoting equal parenting would like to see those questions go away, they are still valid. We just don't know what would happen if we moved tomorrow to a social order in which men did as much childcare as women now do.

We all have clear stereotypes about traditional father figures, and some experience in distinguishing the trustworthy ones from the question marks. But what does a modern, non-authoritarian, child-centred man look like? If you have no model to refer to, how can you decide which one you can trust? If modern father figures present like honorary women, there are the worries that they are too effeminate, too touchy-feely, and so perhaps inclined to abuse. But if they throw themselves about like 'real men', the worry is that they might be inclined to roughness, cruel authoritarianism and violence.

Publicity campaigns for new fathers have a clever way of bypassing these worries, says Jungian analyst Andrew Samuels: they feature only hairless men. Rather than threatening excess eroticism or violence, he says, these images suggest that good new fathers have no testosterone whatsoever.[49] You could say that this is the only way forward, given the present atmosphere of suspicion – a hairless man being better than no man at all.

But it is a cop-out that leaves real fathers with very little room for manoeuvre. It means they must guard against excessive physical tenderness with children, while also reassuring all those around them that they have the 'violence thing' under control too. A mother can talk openly about 'wanting to kill the little darling sometimes', just as she can speak of the bond she feels with her baby as physical, pleasurable and better than sex. She can say these things and be reasonably sure that her comments will be taken in context. Of course people will understand that she is not having a sexual affair with the baby, and that her violent thoughts are just thoughts and so easily controlled. But it is not quite so easy for a man. There is still an extreme cultural nervousness about any close male contact with children. There is much talk in the active fathering movement of giving men time to explore their new terrain, and allowing them to find 'new ways' to be good parents. But real fathers must do so largely without the sort of wide-ranging public discussion that has made such a difference to women who have ventured into traditional male terrain over the past three decades. Even if they do succeed in winning the confidence and respect of their own little circle of friends, they will remain objects of suspicion whenever they venture outside it.

For example – a male friend of mine who has had custody of his son from early infancy cannot take the baby anywhere without someone coming up to him and asking, 'Is that child yours?' Another friend who saw a child alone and crying in the street recently decided to send a woman out to ask if she needed help; he was afraid that if he approached her, someone would suspect him of trying to abduct her. Still another friend, who was taking his daughter to a university interview, talked of his nervousness when checking in to a hotel. 'We were taking separate rooms, but I still had the feeling they weren't sure what I was up to.'

With stepfathers, the suspicions are even worse – as Julia Somerville's partner discovered when he went to Boots to collect some photographs in 1997. The roll included some pictures of his young stepchildren nude. A concerned employee alerted the police and so the man was arrested. His innocence was soon established, and afterwards much outrage was expressed in the tabloid papers about this incident. How dare the authorities hound a nice middle-class man who was so obviously above board! But this little episode did change the way most nice middle-class men took pictures, at least the snapshots they took to Boots. Asked if he minds picking up that roll of film when he's out shopping, it is not unusual for a nice middle-class man to say, 'Aren't those the ones we took at the beach in Greece? If they are, I'd better not go anywhere near them.'

The strangest thing about the campaign to protect children from abusers is that it has grown in tandem with the campaign for active fathering. And yet the two are rarely addressed in one breath. It's as if it's just too disturbing to consider them together, so instead we split them. Active fathers are hairless and angelic. Abusive fathers are hairy, violent, monstrous. And although we have vivid and specific ideas about the things the bad guys do, our ideas about good fathers remain nebulous and negative. They live to fail: at present, the only woman in Britain who can be confident that the father of her child will never let her down is Diane Blood.

3
The Shaky Foundations

The foundations of the new morality

In the first part of this book, we looked at panics that gave a narrative shape to anxieties about modern reproductive strategies. In the second, we took a closer look at the stereotypes that seem to personify all the wrongs of modern family life. In this section, we'll consider the growing anxiety about the foundations of family life.

The stories that fuel this anxiety tend to be sketchy. The few facts on offer hint at darker secrets lurking below the surface, but they are hard to get at. This is one of the reasons why in public discussions these sketchy, suggestive stories move so quickly from the specific to the general. Each new tragedy becomes a reminder that 'the family, the building block of society, is in danger of collapse'.

The magnitude of this danger is evident from the metaphors which writers use to describe it. They talk of shifting sands and sudden shocks, eroding foundations and subterranean shifts and tremors and underlying faults. Above all, they warn of impending disaster. No one can predict when and where the disaster will strike – only that it will happen, and happen without warning; and that when it does, the only people with a hope in hell of surviving are those who have had the foresight to build safe houses.

In the chapters that follow, I consider four chronic anxieties which have made many people talk as if we were living in a moral earthquake zone. These are (1) the growing awareness of child abuse; (2) the growing concern about the long-term effects of family breakdown; (3) the perceived rise in the number of depressed and suicidal children; and (4) the proliferation of panics about bad teenagers. My aim is to show how none of these panics was spontaneous: we owe our present level of anxiety to years of steady campaigning by social action groups. But once a panic enters the public domain, it takes on a life of its own. *These* four panics did much to legitimise the four key ideas that underpin the new morality. The first is that parents should not necessarily have the right to privacy; the second that family breakdown causes children great, lasting and irreversible damage; the third that damaged children turn into the antisocial teenagers who wreck our property and make our streets unsafe, and then go on to perpetuate the misery by having children of their own. The fourth idea is that there is only one way to break this vicious cycle. The only way to stop the teenagers, and save the children, is to target the parents.

Abuse: facts and fantasies

'Video captures attack on baby'. 'Exposing the parents who tortured children'. 'Timetable to abuse'. 'Grim justice by video'. 'Child abuse: the full picture'. These are some of the headlines awarded to the story of Professor David Southall's controversial covert video surveillance of families in which there had been a series of unexplained infant deaths or ill-nesses. The operation began in 1986 at the Royal Brompton Hospital in London, and shifted to Stoke-on-Trent in 1992 where it went on for another two years. All in all, Professor Southall's team observed 39 children aged between 2 and 44 months. The children had a total of 41 siblings, 12 of whom had died 'suddenly and unexpectedly'. Eleven of these had been classified as cot deaths. Many of the parents gave every appearance of being 'caring and kind' in the presence of pro-fessionals. But the moment they were left alone, the videotapes show them turning 'cruel and sadistic'.[1]

I am going to be specific about the things the videotapes show, because later on I will be asking you to question the conclusions people draw from them. But it would be wrong to ask any question that encouraged anyone to make light of the evidence, to evade in any way the fact that we are talking about things that really happened, and could happen again. The tapes make a nonsense of the assumption that there is such a thing as a maternal instinct.

Think of it as a reality check. This is what one video shows going on between an apparently caring and kind mother and a three-month-old daughter who has already been admitted to hospital twice with breathing difficulties. Surveillance begins at 12.24 p.m. Between 2.02 and 2.09 the mother slaps the infant's head three times. At 2.53, she tears up the nursing records. Five minutes later she swears at the child, then kisses her, then makes her vomit. She shakes her roughly, then she tries to calm her for a short while. Then she picks her up by the arms and shakes her. At 3:01, the mother slaps the baby on the face 14 times. At 3.02 she bends her arm back more than 180 degrees. The baby screams; the mother presses the alarm button and tells the nurses the baby has caught her arm on a toy. Thirty seconds after the nurse leaves, the mother bends the arm back again. At 3.06 she is separated from the child.

In the second case, the subject is another girl, aged eighteen months. The surveillance goes on for four days. The mother spends six hours with her child on the first day, but nothing untoward happens. On the second day, she threatens the child with a smack if 'she doesn't stop that noise'. Two hours later, she smacks the child with a toy hammer. She smacks her again a few minutes after that, and later, when her child begins to cry, she pinches her. That evening, when the mother tells her child to go to sleep, she hits her on the back, bottom and leg. On the third day, the mother smacks her child, once because the child has kicked her legs and the other times for no apparent reason. She also scratches her leg. On the fourth day, she slaps her daughter, then hits her on the forehead, then throws toy bricks at her head. Two minutes later, she puts a hand over her child's mouth and slaps her hard on the face. Fifteen minutes after that, she trips the child up and kicks her three times. Then, after she has changed the child's nappy, she takes a pillow, forces it over the child's head, leaves it there for eight seconds, takes it away and then puts it back for another three seconds, at which point a nurse who has been alerted by the observers intervenes.

This was the sort of evidence that led to 38 childcare proceedings and resulted in 33 of the 39 parents being prosecuted. In 30 cases, there was evidence of deliberate suffocation. In other cases, there was evidence of poisoning and deliberate fracture. In a report in the US journal, *Pediatrics*, Professor Southall called for a different approach to child protection. One could not always be open and work with parents, because some parents had personality disorders that made them just too dangerous. The parents whose dangerous behaviour he had caught on videotape were hard to spot by normal means because by and large they came across as 'charming and attractive people'. Sociopaths do not have a sense of right or wrong, but they are well-attuned to what other people respond to as right and wrong: hence their 'ability to evade and deceive professionals as well as the media'. He did not recommend more and better surveillance: he didn't think it necessary. He and his team had been able to compile enough information to come up with a profile of families likely to carry out these horrifying acts. It was particularly important to take a more forensic approach with families in which there had been more than one cot death. 'A proportion of serious child abuse is inflicted by severely disturbed, deceitful but plausible parents,' he wrote. 'This abuse may be difficult to recognise, life-threatening and associated with extreme degrees of physical and mental harm that are difficult to imagine.'[2]

It was not quite as difficult, though, after selected clips were shown on television. 'It doesn't bear thinking about, does it?' wrote a shocked Libby Purves afterwards. But now, faced with such vivid and irrefutable evidence, we had no choice.

There were muted pleas from cot death organisations. Various civil rights groups raised the obvious ethical questions about covert surveillance, the Hippocratic oath and civil rights. Some colleagues accused the professor of exposing the children to risk in order to collect evidence. There were protests from parents, too: as a result of these, Professor Southall was suspended by North Staffordshire Hospital NHS Trust 'pending a number of potentially serious albeit unsubstantiated allegations concerning child protection and research issues at the hospital.'[3] But when the story first broke in 1997, a leader writer at the *Guardian* expressed disappointment that the surveillance was not to continue: 'Professor Southall believes suspect families can now be identified without video evidence. We doubt it. With no hard evidence, diagnosis will be open to wide dispute. There should be a permanent unit to which suspect families should be sent.'[4] Libby Purves expressed similar thoughts: 'Infanticide happens . . . These things are horrible but they are true; we do not have the right to indulge our sentimentality by romanticising motherhood and blinding ourselves to the things that can go sour in women, as well as men . . . if children are to be protected, somebody in the system has to have the kind of suspicious mind which accepts that awful fantasies and cruelties may lurk behind respectable façades. And the rest of us, the vast majority, will have to put up gracefully with the possibility of sharp looks, persistent questions and possible electronic surveillance. Anything is better than the ostrich position, and Dr Southall is right to ask us.'

She ends her column with an account of a health visitor who performed a friendly but overly thorough physical examination of her first-born infant. 'Fascinated, I nerved myself to ask whether she was looking for signs of abuse,' Purves recalls. '"Yes," she said. "You have to. Everywhere. I'm sorry if it offends you. It isn't personal."

'But the odd thing,' Purves went on to confess, 'is that I was not offended, not remotely. I was filled with a wondering, joyful sense of reassurance. This baby, so recently a burden I lumbered around with unaided, was now an independent member of society with his own rights. He would be protected even against me. Call me unmaternal if you like, but it felt good.'[5]

I would never call her unmaternal, and I do know how she feels. When my youngest was two, she had three head injuries in the space of three or four months. None of these accidents happened 'in private'. The first was at her nursery: she tripped and gashed her head against the corner of a low table. The second occurred when her nanny was looking after her and entertaining a friend who had a slightly older son. He was leading my daughter around the kitchen table with a tie from a bathrobe, and at one point he tugged at it sharply, causing her to fall and crack her chin. A month later, she was coming down a chute at a soft play centre when she knocked heads with an unsupervised child who had decided to crawl in to the chute at the bottom, and whom I was not able to remove from harm's way in time. My daughter had a bump the size of an egg, and so we took her to Casualty to make sure she was all right, just as we had done on the two earlier occasions. When my health visitor heard of these visits, she subjected me to a very unfriendly grilling. It was an extremely unpleasant experience, because if someone suspects you of child cruelty, it is very difficult to provide her with reasons why she should trust you. All I could do was tell her that there had been other witnesses in all three instances, and that she should not rely on what I said but should also consult them. Despite my discomfort, I thought she was right to ask me questions. I was willing to endure her high and mighty looks if it meant that the same procedure would be in place in cases where children were truly at risk. I was, of course, confident that she would eventually come to believe me.

The proper management of the abusers is a source of comfort to all those who care about child welfare. It's through the policing of the aberrant extremes that the values of normal, healthy, happy child-rearing are made visible and so reaffirmed.

But *are* we doing a sufficiently good job of policing these aberrant extremes? The ever-rising numbers of child abuse and neglect cases in the news cannot help but make us wonder. Think of all those mothers who virtually handed over their young daughters to violent and sadistic boyfriends. Then remember Ruth Neave, the drug addict who was cleared of strangling her son Rikki and abandoning him in the woods, but who was jailed for 7 years in 1997 after being convicted of five charges of cruelty to him as well as to two of his sisters. Ruth had burned one daughter's hand with a cigarette and squirted washing-up liquid down Rikki's throat. Early one December morning, when Rikki was three, she had pushed him out of the house wearing nothing but his pyjamas.[6]

Consider Michelle Jones, who raised an alarm about her missing three-year-old daughter in November 1998. Police found Charlotte 29 hours later, not quite dead of exposure, sitting 'cold and damp under a curtain of brambles' in a nearby copse. Not long afterwards, Michelle appeared before Warrington magistrates accused of wilfully abandoning Charlotte and maliciously causing her daughter grievous bodily harm.[7]

That same week, a woman named Tracey Nolan who had gone on holiday to Turkey with her husband and children from both his and her previous marriages – and who had then run off with a Middle Eastern businessman, taking her children with her – decided (for reasons unknown) that the children were better off without her. So she popped them into a taxi with only just enough money to cover the fare to the British consulate in Istanbul. When they arrived, the consulate was closed. They had to stay with a guard until it reopened.[8]

Can we call each one of these stories exceptional, or do they indicate a new trend? Tracey Nolan is hardly the only mother to make the papers this decade by abandoning her children for a taste of the good life. The gold standard was set by the infamous 'home alone' mothers like the one who went off on a holiday to Benidorm in September 1995, leaving her three children to their own devices. A concerned neighbour alerted police and social services sixteen hours after her departure. When they arrived, they found the 12-year-old girl cooking chips for her 5- and 7-year-old brothers.[9]

In this case, the children were taken off to be better cared for by relatives. The six-month-old baby whom 23-year-old Antoinette Campbell left alone for 30 hours the following November was not quite so lucky. Campbell was given probation, as the cause of death was uncertain.[10] In another case from that same year, a mother whose toddler died while unattended did get a sentence, but it was only fifteen months. She had left the 21-month-old girl in the care of her other daughter, aged six. While she was having a few drinks at a local working men's club, the toddler found a substance similar to amyl nitrate on the kitchen table and drank it. The six-year-old carried her out into the street to get some help, but her sister, whom neighbours reported as looking very grey, died before she reached hospital.[11] The mother was said to be beside herself, was receiving treatment for depression, and had taken a number of overdoses.

In August 1998, we heard that the number of new mothers abandoning their children had trebled in ten years. In 1986, police recorded 22 mothers abandoning a child under two. In 1996, there were 65 cases. According to Dr Lorraine Sherr of the Royal Free Hospital, London, most abandoning mothers do go out of their way to ensure the children are safe: 'They will wrap their baby in a blanket or leave a note, or call 999 from a call-box to say they've found a baby and check the baby is found.' Only very rarely did they 'leave their baby under a bush or in a bag'.[12]

Nevertheless, these bush and bag cases are the ones most likely to get into the news. Here's one from December 1998: 'Baby Under Bush Saved By Mild Night.' It was, in fact, one of the mildest December nights on record. The baby had probably been lying under the holly bush for six hours when the owners of the house found him naked and suffering from hypothermia. He did reach hospital in time, and so was expected to recover. The photographs that accompanied the report followed the usual iconic rules for such incidents, with the fragile infant in the centre, and in the arms of a haggard but visibly trustworthy female saviour. In this case, it was Nurse Jane Bennett. Asked for her thoughts on the episode, she kept to gracious convention by focusing attention on the infant. 'He's gorgeous. His mother must have been desperate.'[13]

Reports also carried a plea to the mother to get in touch, and a promise that she would receive a sympathetic hearing. In most cases, abandoned babies are reunited with their mothers 'with appropriate support'. According to Felicity Collier of the British Agencies for Adoption and Fostering, both the mothers and their children suffer 'dreadfully' if this doesn't happen.[14]

In saying this, she was reflecting a central tenet of our child protection services, as they're now framed: that it's essential to foster and support the mother-child relationship whenever possible, because families are almost always the best places for rearing children. This is the assumption that Professor Southall was challenging when he subjected us to video evidence of parenting behind closed doors. It was a focused and specific challenge: he was saying that there were some parents who could not be trusted, and who had been hard to identify in the past, but who would be easier to identify in future thanks to his pioneering research. He was not implying that his discoveries were just the tip of the iceberg. But other people do.

One such person is Professor Southall's long-time associate, Sir Roy Meadows. Formerly of the Department of Paediatrics and Child Health at St James's Hospital in Leeds, and recently retired, he continues to be one of our leading authorities on child abuse, particularly abuse perpetrated by mothers like those in the Southall study who suffer from Munchausen syndrome-by-proxy. In January 1999, he published an article in the medical journal *Archives of Childhood*, in which he examined the cases of 81 children who were originally diagnosed as having died either of natural causes or SIDS (cot death), and whose parents were later convicted of murder. In almost all these cases, the killer had been the mother and the method had been suffocation. In five cases where the original certificate gave SIDS as the cause of death, the children were over a year old – despite the fact that the upper limit for SIDS is six months. Two of these 81 children had fractured bones; 27 had blood in the mouth, nose or on the face at the time of death, and ten had unusual bruises on the face and neck. Still others had coins, balls of paper and mittens in their airways or intestines. And yet somehow the coroners and pathologists had not seen these things as cause for concern.

Sir Roy Meadows blamed the system for these dangerous oversights. Coroners and pathologists were under pressure to arrive at a quick decision, and hospitals and paediatricians were not at all good at spotting children at risk. Nearly half the children in his study had been taken to hospital by their mothers in the week before they died. 'If a young child is admitted to hospital as a result of a young, harassed mother from a poor home recounting a startling or unusual event, it does not mean all is well . . . That mother has brought the child to hospital for a reason that we have not understood.' He went on to imply that we have not understood these women because we do not want to believe that mothers who give out all the right signals might be secretly trying to murder their children. 'SIDS has been used, at times, as a pathological diagnosis to evade awkward truths,' he said. 'If one out of every thousand 21-year-olds died suddenly and unexpectedly without an identifiable cause there would be a national outcry.' It was, he said, a 'national scandal that we accept a situation in which so many young children die of unknown causes'.[15]

In fact, there has been a steep drop in the number of cot deaths in the past thirty years. In 1971 there were 1,500. Now we average 400 a year. It's thought that the main reason for this drop is the campaign to stop parents letting their babies sleep on their tummies. It's hard to know how many of the remaining cases are genuine cot deaths – for all the reasons Sir Roy Meadows outlined, these cases touch on something that few of us want to acknowledge. And then there's the 'problem' of a parent's right to privacy. David Southall's own research was hampered after complaints by parents led to West Midlands Health Authority deciding to investigate his use of video surveillance. He and his colleagues hoped that the BMA's decision to set up a working party would lead to clear guidelines and a greater public understanding of MSBP. But before the public could really grasp what MSBP was all about, he said, it would first have to decide what mattered most – parents' rights or a 'child's right to live free from abuse'.[16]

Put that way, it is only too clear what matters most. A child has a right to humane treatment. A parent who slams the door to prying outsiders in order to abuse a child is abusing not just the child but the very right to privacy. It would be hard to argue that emergency tactics are never necessary to rescue children from parents who are putting their lives at risk. But when the problem is framed like this, as an undefined menace lurking behind doors slammed shut by abusers who look totally normal, the very idea of a normal parent becomes problematic.

Just how problematic was only too clear to the grieving parents of genuine cot death victims after Sir Roy Meadows' research made the headlines last January. Anne Deri-Bowen, the national coordinator of the Foundation for the Study of Infant Deaths, told the *Guardian* that many parents had been phoning their help-line to talk of their distress about the way the findings were being reported. Although one mother went into her children's school building so that she could avoid the other parents at the gate, another mother had come up to her to say, 'Don't worry. I know you didn't kill the baby.' Another mother, Juliet Hughes-Hallett, said that the reports had prompted her three children, all born after her first daughter died of SIDS seventeen years ago, to ask for the very first time for details of the tragedy: 'They wanted to know, "technically", what Emily died of.'

'The fact is when you've lost a baby in a cot death, your first feelings are of guilt. It's inevitable. You arrive at the hospital with your baby, then you go home without the baby.' But the doubts stay with you: 'With every new piece of research you ask yourself, was she too hot, or did we have her facing the wrong way?'

'Never,' she says. 'The grief never goes.' The effects of cot death on a family, says Julia Samuel, co-founder of the Child Bereavement Trust, are 'deep-rooted' and long-lasting. 'A parent's gut response is, "I am responsible for keeping my baby safe and well."' Acknowledging that they 'probably aren't responsible, while simultaneously recognising that they feel responsible, helps them to grasp a better piece of truth'.[17]

All this implies a sympathetic listener - a listener who is willing to believe they are innocent, even as she reminds herself that innocence is not something she can blindly count on. This fine balancing of an open mind is not possible in a culture of suspicion. In such a culture, all concerned citizens think like private investigators and all parents are, at least in theory, potential killers.

The crusade to protect children from incompetent, abusive or neglectful parents has a long and chequered history. As one legal historian puts it, our awareness of child abuse has 'cycled between discovery and invisibility, panic and indiffer-ence'. Our definitions have changed just as dramatically, she says, and have included crimes as diverse as 'exposure to the elements, exposure to immorality, physical and emotional neglect, corporal punishment, incest, sexual assault, sexual exploitation, foetal damage, transracial or transcultural adoption, ritual or satanic abuse'.[18]

The cures change in accordance with the diagnosis. Over the last hundred years, they have ranged from the lecturing or tutoring of parents, and the apprehension or institutionalisa-tion of the children, to public education drives, poverty relief, day-care provision, the improvement of educational and social facilities, and 'visionary calls for massive social reform or revolution'.[19]

The convention is to assign root causes that fit in with larger social or political prejudices. In the late nineteenth century, when feminists joined other moral crusaders here and in the US to campaign against cruelty to children, the vogue was to see it as a moral problem that resided in the 'bestiality' of lower-class males and what were seen to be the 'inadequacies' of poor or immigrant mothers. In the early years of the twentieth century, the new armies of social work-ers offered an alternative to this diet of moral condemnation. To them, abuse was not a moral failing but an illness. Then, as sociologists arrived on the scene to challenge the medical model, we began to look at abusers more as products of their environment. Then, with the feminist 'rediscovery' of incest, men became the problem again, except that this time it was not just lower-class men but all men who were prepared to defend patriarchal privilege with violence. But now, the fem-inist campaigns have merged with the medical and psychiatric campaigns they helped to inspire. The root causes have mul-tiplied. Abusers can be seeking power or they can be sexually dysfunctional. They can be products of their environment and also be mentally ill. They can be men or they can be women. But no matter what they are, and what has prompted them to become abusers, the thing which the new abuse campaigners believe they abuse most is their right to privacy. It is to challenge the place where the law draws the line that they work so hard to 'raise awareness' about the unknown numbers of children who are still out there and at risk.

The definition of that risk is infinitely expandable – as we can see from an Office of National Statistics survey that was released in June 1999. For the first time ever, the survey linked the death certificates of children under four with their birth certificates, and so includes information about their parents' age at the time of their births as well as their parents' occupation, marital status, social class and country of origin. One finding was that babies born out of wedlock to women who were not living with the father were much more likely to die before the age of four than were babies whose parents cohabited. This could have something to do with the fact that most of the women who fit into this category live in poverty. Indeed, it probably would not be difficult to use data from the ONS survey to make this case. But it was the marital status of mothers that sparked national interest. The headline in the *Guardian* was 'Fatherless Babies Face Death Risks'.[20]

An article that ran a few weeks later detailed the health risks suffered by children whose parents smoked. They were five times more likely to suffer cot death.[21] Once again, the other factors were not mentioned. For example, parents living in poverty are more likely to smoke than are middle-class parents.

You could, if you wished, argue that poverty is the single most important risk factor for children, all across the board. A child living in poverty is less likely to do well in school and to prosper in later life, more likely to suffer poor health,

depression, homelessness – you name it. I am sure David
Southall and Sir Roy Meadows are right when they say that
people just don't want to know about the true extent of child
abuse, but I am just as sure that the main thing we do not
wish to face as a society is that the greatest child abuser of
them all is poverty. We don't want to know this, because it
would be too expensive to fix. Far better to be economical
with the truth, and blame the parents.

Passing the buck like this is not just unfair but also unpro-
ductive. Blanket condemnations do not encourage clear
thought or careful observation. They impose a conclusion
and so make it harder to tell the difference between the parents who do harm their children and those who do not. Even
worse, they create an alarmist parent-bashing climate that
makes it very dangerous for any parent to admit in public
what we all know privately: there are many ways in which
normal modern family life really does cause children terrible
grief.

Don't look now: divorce and the struggle to save marriage

What is the most heartrending divorce story you've ever
heard? This is one of mine. It begins when Peter Malkin, self-
made businessman, kidnaps Oliver Malkin, his son. After
some time, they are traced to a resort in Egypt. The son is said
to be happy, the father defiant. The father's British assets are
frozen. He is sent a psychiatrist's report warning of harm he is
causing his son. He promises to return to the UK, but when
he gets to Heathrow he makes a scene. Later, he is sentenced
to eighteen months for defying the court order not to take
Oliver away from his mother, Elisa Pridmore. But the press
are on his side and give him headlines like 'How a Father's

Desperation led to an Act of Madness'. When Peter Malkin walks out of court, he tells reporters: 'I love Oliver. I wish him the best. Send all my love to Oliver – just my love.'[22]

Before the Peter Malkin trial hit the news and after it faded, the standard view was that the rise in the divorce rate was a sign of mass moral failure. Divorce was something that people did because they were lazy, egocentric, or out for a life of easy pleasures, and therefore something that they might stop doing if they could somehow be made to take their responsibilities seriously. But no one in his right mind would dream of accusing Peter Malkin of indolence. He had gone to extraordinary lengths to stay in touch with his son since the boy's mother remarried and decamped with him to Brittany. In six years, he had kidnapped Oliver four times. The first time was in 1987, the year of the divorce, when he picked up Oliver after school and managed to keep him hidden for six months. The police eventually found him in a secret attic room at Malkin's hotel in Devon. It was after this that Oliver's mother thought it prudent to move to France. But that only seems to have renewed his father's resolve to assert his authority as the British father of a British boy. Once he went so far as to enlist the help of a masked gang that sprayed CS gas at the family dogs; on that occasion, he took Oliver on a 19-month tour of Europe and North Africa. This last time, he had arranged to spend Christmas with Oliver in Egypt by pulling up alongside the boy and his grandmother as they walked home from his school in Brittany and (with the help of his fiancée and another man) bundling the boy into the car. Not all went according to plan: the grandmother was still attached to the car when they tried to drive off, and so they ended up dragging her some way down the road.

This final escapade had cost him dearly. He had risked everything he owned just to have some time with his son, to be his father. And just to be his father, he had also done terrible damage to the boy's schooling. By now, Oliver had missed an equivalent of three years' tuition: he was having to make it up with private tutors. And that was just the beginning, his mother said when she appeared on 'Frost on Sunday'. 'Each time he was kidnapped, it was violent, and that sort of trauma does leave its mark on a child.' She thought he would have to see counsellors, and would end up being 'scarred for life'. She expressed relief at the sentence: her family would be able to breathe again. For six years they had lived in fear. Oliver needed some breathing space, too. He was 'sensitive, vulnerable, needy, and in colloquial terms, a mess'. It would be good to get him back home again, where he could 'play with his friends like a normal child without wondering if his father and the heavies are going to turn up and snatch him'. She said she had always supported her son if he wanted to have access to Peter. The problem was that Oliver felt 'very dominated by his natural father. He doesn't trust his father, which is very sad. I think he is happy with the family he has now.'[23]

What she thought about her ex-husband, she was careful not to say. She did not press charges against her ex-husband's fiancée. She said nothing to the press when a month into his imprisonment he applied for care and control of Oliver or reasonable access. She did not complain about the somewhat partisan coverage of her ex-husband's transfer from Pentonville prison to Canterbury. (The poor man looked 'dishevelled', we read, and was 'shaky on his feet'.)[24] She said nothing when he complained to the press about how difficult it was for Oliver to visit him in prison. Not wishing to 'fan the flames' (as a friend of hers put it), she kept her silence when Peter was finally freed in September after serving eight months. Peter, too, was careful to say only positive things. Jubilant as he embraced his fiancée, he told a group of reporters that it was 'quite wonderful to be in the open air'.

He was never going to kidnap Oliver again. And yes, things were still fine between them. 'He loves me as I love him.'[25]

It is extraordinary, when you think about all the laws he broke in the name of this love, that he enjoyed the degree of public support he did. The accounts of his exploits are suffused with pity, compassion and awe. There are feature articles that seek to put his tragedy in context. We hear that 900 fathers abducted their children in 1993. We are told that the law is stacked against them, and that it's time to address their grievances.[26] 'The current legislation encourages abduction,' said Jasmine Salisbury in a letter to the *Independent*. Although it was true that a father who was denied contact could in theory take the mother to court, in real life he was powerless if she refused to comply. The legal guarantees were 'merely a sop to Cerberus'. What court would send the mother of a small child to prison?[27]

No one alluded directly to the distress he must have felt at his son growing up in France, but it did seem to add another dimension to the tragedy. This was a man whose son had been appropriated not just by another man, but by another culture. But not for long: a year later, we heard that Peter Malkin had again applied for custody of his son, now 14, following the death of his mother. 'It's absolutely rotten that Elisa died like this,' he told reporters on the eve of his application to the High Court.[28] When Mr Justice Kirkwood granted him custody six weeks later, in accordance with the boy's wishes, he behaved, as always, like a larger-than-life gentleman. He assured the court that Oliver would 'remain in close contact with members of his late mother's family who are dear to him. These are distressing days for Oliver as he mourns his mother and faces making major adjustments in his life.'[29]

And with that, Peter Malkin and his son disappeared from the news, taking a very large unanswered question with them.

What *was* it that had prompted this man to take such desperate action? It was impossible to know, and so it was easy to
assume that this story was just another Greek tragedy, just
another story in which people got divorced, went mad and
wreaked havoc.

Why weren't we doing more to restore order, keep these
things from getting out of hand? In fact, the Lord Chancellor's
Department had been doing quite a lot, in its fashion. The
Children Act 1989, held that a child's views should be taken
into account in deciding what happened to them when their
parents separated, but had not done much to change the
status quo. The same went for the 1990 UN Convention on
the Rights of the Child. It, too, held that a child's voice should
be heard wherever feasible, and that *all* parents be supported
in their efforts to bring up their children. But that had not
done much to alter things either. In 1991 we got the Child
Support Act – designed, we were promised, to take care of all
those fathers who had abandoned their children and their
children's mothers to a lifetime on income support.
'Parenthood is for life,' said Margaret Thatcher at the launch
for the Child Support Agency. But life is complicated, and so
was the formula the CSA used when setting the levels of support.

It made a series of catastrophic mistakes. Blameless husbands faced the wrath of blameless wives when letters arrived
telling them to pay more than they earn for children they'd
never heard of. Others received demands to pay so much for
their children from their first family that their second families
would be left with nothing. Many of the mothers in whose
name the CSA was making claims were as angry as the
fathers. Either they said they wanted no link and no contact
whatsoever with these men, or they said it was hard enough
to keep the peace with them already, without the added strain
of a pay demand that was likely to be based on faulty data.

When some fathers got organised to fight the new law, there was derision from certain women in the media, but their taunts did not lead to anyone saying anything in defence of the CSA.

Meanwhile, the 'wars of the roses' escalated. In the *Times* Index for 1990, articles on divorce and separation take up two and a half columns. By 1994, this has risen to five. Running concurrently with the Malkin story in January of that year is a nationwide search for another father who failed to return his two sons to his mother after a New Year's access visit. The mother thinks he's taken them to Florida. When he turns up in Spain, he pledges to return the boys. The courts freeze his assets anyway, just in case. Then attention turns to yet another alert at all ports and airports for a father who has snatched his son and may be heading for Turkey. The next day, a father in a child custody case kidnaps a Canadian family in a 'bizarre' attempt to get his own children returned to him. Two weeks on, the bodies of a father and three daughters at the centre of a custody dispute are found in a fume-filled car.

Then there's a national alert following the kidnapping of a baby boy 'by two men believed to be his father and grandfather'. A Derby woman is reunited with her children nine months after her estranged Greek-Cypriot husband abducted them. An inquest is told how a bullied schoolgirl committed suicide after her parents' marriage broke up. Another inquest hears that the father who killed himself and his daughters was seeking revenge on his wife. The father of a multiple transplant girl who died has to take his wife to court to get access to their two surviving sons.

A Rochdale woman is one of ten mothers flown to Libya at the invitation of the country's leader to see children abducted by estranged Libyan fathers: she discovers that her son has forgotten how to speak English. Extradition papers are prepared to return to Britain a woman who fled to Australia with her 'tug of love' son. A father loses his appeal in the High Court to take his children away from their lesbian mother. An escaped prisoner abducts his children from his first marriage with the help of his second wife. There is an eleven-hour siege. It ends peacefully – but no one's sighing with relief.[30]

Because during that same year, we've been told about a study showing that children whose parents divorce can suffer behavioural problems for years afterwards and do less well at school than they should. Another study suggests that stormy marriages may do children less harm than 'amicable' divorces. Yet another reminds us that children from broken families suffer from low self-esteem. A European study shows that attempted suicide is more likely in families where parents are divorced or separated. Another reveals that even children in 'stable' families live in terror of their parents splitting.

As plans for the Family Law Bill proceed, there is much discussion of the ever-rising divorce rate, and the also-rising number of children being born out of wedlock. There are attacks on the idea of marriage as a contract, and warnings about what happens to the weaker member of the union if this contract can be dissolved too quickly. There are arguments about the merits and demerits of prenuptial agreements, counselling, mediation, shared custody, and divorced women having a share of their ex-husbands' pensions. There is the Irish referendum and there is the gossip about the disintegrating royal marriages. We find out about life after divorce: what it's like to sell your house, how many friends you lose, how poor women get and how bad it is for men's health, but no amount of bad news about divorce is enough to stop the epidemic. Marriage, we read, is at a fifty-year low, and divorce rates are at an all-time high. No one can quite explain why this is so, but as the decade progresses, more and more people start trying.

This is easier said than done, because there are so very many factors. A recent review of research commissioned by One Plus One for the Lord Chancellor's Department found that people who married very young were at higher risk of getting divorced, but the same held true for those who lived together before they got married, those who had lived with other people before living together, those whose own parents had divorced, and those who had children before they got married or who had 'short first birth intervals'.[31]

But the same report admits that the statistics are inadequate, especially for people who cohabit rather than marry. Many new studies are forced to depend on twenty-year-old data which is very bad news when you are trying to grapple with new, hard-to-predict trends such as cohabitation. Judging from studies in other countries, it does seem likely that cohabiting couples are far less stable than married couples. No one knows how much this has to do with the fact that people who choose to cohabit 'feel less commitment' from the very beginning, and how much these figures tell you about the stabilising features of 'the institution of marriage'.[32]

According to the German social theorists Ulrich Beck and Elisabeth Beck-Gernsheim, figures like this can't tell you much anyway, because their scope is too narrow and superficial. They are of the view that the primary agent of marriage erosion is the labour market, or rather 'the failure of a family model' which can only work if one adult works outside the home and one remains based inside it, but which cannot accommodate two wage slaves since this will oblige both partners 'to put themselves first'.

The traditional family, they go on to say, does not fit in with modern life. As an institution, it has never been democratic; is still, they say, 'semi-feudal'. Despite the lip service both men and women pay to equality, the old ideas about paternal privilege and maternal sacrifice run deep. If you look at the larger social issues that play themselves out inside modern marriages, it becomes clear that the high divorce rate is just one way in which a central contradiction in our way of life plays itself out.

It may be that the problems of modern marriage are so big that only the happiest and most fortunate couples will ever be able to solve them. Even so, divorce stories can offer some insight into the marriages that preceded them. People tend to think of marriage and divorce as two separate entities, but in many ways divorces are just continuations of what came before. Divorces offer insight into fault lines of modern marriage. Promoting the virtues of marriage, seeking to renew or modernise this institution without first coming to terms with its evident faults seems to me to be absurd.

However, this is not the view of most right-wing anti-divorce campaigners. The same holds true for the (mostly American) communitarians who are now at the forefront of the marriage renewal movement. Instead of seeing marriage and divorce on a continuum, they prefer to divide the world into two camps. The people in the first camp are virtuous, hard-working, beleaguered, but still working hard at their demanding marriages, while those in the second camp are slackers who exert a terrible influence not just over their own children but over society in general, by putting their own selfish needs first and getting divorced.

The American communitarian Barbara Dafoe Whitehead went to great lengths to promote this view in her book, *The Divorce Culture*. The polluting effect of the rising divorce rate was, she claimed, America's best-kept secret. Americans were refusing to face this fact because it was in the interests of many important people that they remain in the dark. She attributed the long 'conspiracy of silence' on the ravages of divorce to the large numbers of divorced men in positions of power and influence. They didn't want to think about it because this time it was not a Them Problem (e.g. something they could blame on the underclass) but an Us Problem. She used teen fiction (fiction written by adults *for* teens, that is) to gauge the unacknowledged distress children suffer, and she quoted from upbeat self-help books to support her claim that the vast majority of divorces were initiated by shallow, selfish people in search of easy gratification. She pointed scathingly to statistics showing that women report they are happier in themselves after divorce, and then equally scathingly to other well-known figures that made a nonsense of their happiness – it was evident that women came out of divorce with their standard of living drastically lowered, so how could they possibly be happier? Like others, she pointed out that the no-fault divorce laws have impacted terribly on women and children, and greatly benefited men. And like those others, she traced this injustice to a legal, economic and social system that honours and rewards cut-throat individualism.[33]

Although she showed that as a rule it was men – and especially rich, powerful men – who benefited from the divorce culture, and women – both dependants and those who worked – who suffered from it, she was reluctant to ask if the same thing might not be so of 'marriage culture' as presently defined. She shares this blind spot with her fellow communitarians, Amitai Etzioni and William Galston: for them, a stable marriage is the best possible place for rearing a child. They avoid the question of fairness, justice and democracy within marriage by assuming it is already democratic enough. And so do their colleagues Jean Bethke Elshtain and Mary Ann Glendon. When they call for a renewal of civic virtue and commitment, when they point out that all parents must make sacrifices, they do not stop to remember that tradition calls for mothers to make the lion's share of sacrifices.

The standard communitarian line on marriage is that it is a flawed institution, but one worth preserving, because it was the best thing we have. But that – most communitarians would agree – still leaves the biggest job undone: how to make these heavier commitments attractive to people? It's not just in the US and Britain that the marriage culture is in decline: it's also happening (at different rates, and to differing degrees) in every country in the industrialised world.

Why do so many people want to avoid it? In the marriage renewal business, the consensus is that they're . . . well . . . irresponsible. They avoid staying married for life 'because they *can* avoid it' or because 'they feel a lower level of commitment'. Deeper investigations into the reasons for marriage failure are similarly judgmental. To fail to remain married is to expose a character flaw. It's fear of abandonment, say the attachment theory people. It's repressed internal models of early childhood carers, assert the object relations brigade, while the cognitive-behaviourists maintain it's the way people argue.

Reading the literature on divorce if you've actually been through a divorce yourself is like playing 'Murder in the Dark.' Now you hit against something that seems to have some substance; then you see something you think you recognise; then you've lost your bearings altogether. No, it wasn't like that at all, you say. The next minute, you're thinking, what if I had a repressed internal model of my mother all along and never knew it? Then you think, I was never as selfish as that. And then you ask yourself, 'Well, maybe I was a bit selfish, but he was still the one in the wrong.'

Most of all, you wonder why there is so little interest in what divorced parents and their children have to say about life after divorce. Why there is such an obsession with the reasons for and the mechanics of marriage breakdown, and then . . . zip. Why our primary function, after our marriages are pronounced dead, seems to be to serve as scarecrows, there to deter others from following in our footsteps. The moral of the Malkin case, the moral of all divorce sagas, is, 'Go this way, and your children will be torn in half.'

But who is responsible for doing the tearing? Received opinion puts it all down to the 'divine madness' that afflicts divorcing couples. But all too often, the tragedy takes place in Family Court. For those of you who are not acquainted with them, Family Courts are closed courts. Not even the court users have access to the files. In disputes between divorced parents over residency and contact, they are expected to reflect the principles set out by the Children Act. This holds that, wherever possible, both parents should be involved in the caring and rearing of the child. The ratios are left to the Court Welfare Officer to decide, and they are meant to be 'within reason'. But there are no guidelines as to what the term 'within reason' really means. The Court Welfare Officers, who belong to the probation service, seem to receive no special training for this job.

Here are a few case histories that might make you want to look again at the Peter Malkin story. I must stress that I have no idea what actually happened between Malkin and his wife during his marriage, and no idea what caused the divorce or what happened afterwards. I am only mapping out the realm of the possible as dictated by the laws and the courts as they are today. In the stories that follow, I have changed all the names.

So first let's look at the case of Richard, a major in the Army and the father of two children. He was devoted to their mother, despite the fact that she was given to violence – she even attacked him with a knife on more than one occasion. One day, she attacked him in the street and a bystander called the police. Furious, the wife ran off, left the children with an unknown friend and told Richard that he would never see his children again. Divorce proceedings began soon afterwards. Because he was concerned that his children might not be safe with their mother, Richard's first plan was to apply for residency, but his solicitors convinced him that he was better off applying for reasonable contact.

He got it, but once the divorce was final it soon became clear that his ex-wife was not intending to cooperate. One weekend when she did let him see them, he found that his daughter was covered with bruises and took her to the hospital at once. They were very concerned about the bruises, which they said were at least two days old; this meant that it was his ex-wife who had inflicted them. She was furious when she discovered he had gone to the authorities, and has refused to abide with the contact agreement since that time.

The court has done nothing to stand in her way. This probably has something to do with the allegations she has made against him, but it may also be associated with the fact that she has friends in the court that heard the case. It is impossible to know for sure because, as I already mentioned, the files in these courts are closed and there is no complaints procedure in place if court users believe that justice has not been done. The only thing they are allowed to complain about is the Court Welfare Officer's body language and tone of voice.

After the marriage ended, Richard found out that his ex-wife had a sixteen-year record of violence and psychiatric problems; she had files with the police and social services and mental health services. After all contact with his children ceased, he happened to see her driving down the high street in her car. One of his daughters was in the back seat and when she saw Richard, she waved. Richard crossed the street to ask his ex-wife if it might be all right to speak to his daughter. Her response was to put the car into reverse, and then into first, in order to run him over. Despite the fact that there were witnesses to this event, the courts have continued to allow her to keep the children and deny Richard all contact. The judge explained his decision by saying that, all things being equal, children under five were much better off with their mothers. What Richard would like to know is, how unequal do things have to be before a judge will override that prejudice?

How typical is that story? And how many excluded parents have, like Richard, suffered nervous breakdowns as a result? It's hard to say, because in the twenty years since the Family Court system began – and despite the fact that half a million cases have gone through them – there has not been a single follow-up study. This may explain why the Family Court experience comes as such a shock to so many parents. As Owen put it, one minute you're sitting on your sofa watching television with your children, telling yourself all is right in the world, and the next minute you're out on the street and someone's telling you that you may never be allowed to see them again.

When Owen split up with the mother of his then six-month-old son, the original agreement was that he would see him every other weekend. But the mother often changed the arrangements at the last minute. This led to an argument, and it was after this argument that the mother refused to allow him any contact at all. She then went to social services and alleged that he had taken their son swimming and tried to drown him. This was found to be untrue, but when Owen took the case to Family Court, the allegation was mentioned many times. At one point in the proceedings, the judge required him to promise never to take his son swimming again. When Owen refused, he was asked to promise never to allow his son's head to go under the water again when taking him swimming. When Owen refused again, he asked him to promise never to force his son's head under water against his will, and he agreed because (he said) this was not something he would ever want to do anyway. During the court case, the mother made a host of other allegations against him. These ranged from fears that he had abused their child during the time he had contact, to fears that he might serve the child cheese sauce if he ever got to see him again. After two years of legal battles, Owen won his case. Since that time, he has had no trouble with contact. Despite all the horrible allegations the mother of his child made against him, relations are so friendly that he can even go into her sitting room when he is returning the child, for a leisurely chat. 'She doesn't have to worry,' says Richard, 'because she knew they were not true. The only reason she made them was to strengthen her case.'

A woman we'll call Rosa is not likely to ever see such a happy outcome. Her marriage ended seven years ago when her husband beat her up for the last time and left home in the middle of the night, taking with him the older of their children, a girl then aged six. When she filed for divorce, it was her original aim to apply for the daughter to be returned to her. But the husband was not friendly to the idea, neither were his mother and sister. After the solicitor told her it was too great a risk to apply for residency, she applied instead for reasonable contact, and she was successful.

Six weeks after the divorce was final, her daughter found her father dead in the shower. By the time Rosa discovered this, the girl was in the care of her paternal grandmother and her aunt. Following advice that seems to have come from friends who worked in the court system, the grandmother had applied for residency. According to documents that Rosa saw much later, the application was supported by vague allegations of abuse. From this moment onwards, Rosa has not been able to see her child, in spite of many efforts on the part of the judge in the case requiring the grandmother to allow contact. The court has done nothing, however, to force her to change her ways. For a while, the grandmother did allow Rosa's younger child to stay in touch with his sister; the condition was that she be present throughout the visit, which should take place at her house. The boy would come home to Rosa looking very upset and it would later emerge that the grandmother had told him, for example, that his mother was a criminal, and that if he stayed with her he would end up getting arrested by the police. On one occasion they told him that his mother was like a chocolate onion – sweet on the outside, but if you bit into it, quite another matter.

In all these cases, there were efforts on the part of the resident parent or guardian to prejudice children against the other parent. In many cases, the hate campaign worked. In the US, the term for this is 'parent alienation syndrome'. To date, it is not a term that carries much weight with the Family Court Welfare Service (soon to be renamed the Children and Family Court Advisory Service). Parents can deliberately alienate their children and be taken at face value. They can refuse to allow the other parent any contact even when the court has made a contact order, and the court does nothing to stand in their way. Despite all the pronouncements about how important it is for a child to stay in regular contact with both parents, the Family Court Welfare Service seems to think that the most important thing is to 'resolve the conflict'. If this means excluding the non-resident parent permanently, then so be it.

The classic media cartoon about life after marriage goes like this: the man walks off, the woman is left to bring up the children on her own. Within the year, the man will have ceased all contact with his children. The truth of the matter is that many of these fathers do not keep up contact with their children because they are not allowed to do so. There are fewer non-resident mothers who find themselves excluded from their children's lives. Even so, this is a tragedy which can happen to women too. But as Rosa, Owen and Richard all insist, the ones who are bound to suffer the most, and the longest, are the children.

And yet there has been no public outcry. When children of broken families feature in the news, they too serve as cautionary tales. This is only too evident in the public response to Monica Cockett and John Tripp's 1994 study of family breakdown and its impact on children, usually known as the Exeter Family Study. This was a small pilot study in which researchers spoke to 152 children from two age groups (9–10 and 13–14) and to their parents. Half lived with both their biological parents in 'intact' families, and the other half lived in families 're-ordered' by separation or divorce.

Its most controversial finding was that children whose parents had divorced amicably did not fare as well as children who still lived with their biological parents in 'high-conflict' marriages. In its conclusion, it set this in the context of other research showing that, while there were exceptions, children in re-ordered families generally had poorer self-esteem, more day-to-day problems with their health, their friends and their schoolwork, less promising long-term and educational prospects, and a greater chance of their own marriages and relationships being short-lived and superficial. It repeated the usual horror statistics: every year, 150,000 children under the age of sixteen are involved in the breakdown of their parents' marriages, and this without counting the many children whose parents go through the same process outside marriage.

The press portrayed the report as further proof that divorce was bad for children, and so to be discouraged, while marriage was good for children and so to be strengthened. As usual, the 'How can it be strengthened?' question got left out of it, as did the related question, 'Just because marriage is better than divorce for children, can we really say it's just right as it is?'

But the thrust of the study itself was very different. The

researchers were interested in finding out what divorce was like for children – what it was really, *really* like – because they thought this input would indicate how to support them better. It made a number of recommendations for minimising the effects of divorce on children. For example, it was clear that children appreciated, and needed, a full explanation from both parents early on. They also needed chances to express their views. After the divorce, they needed opportunities to see both parents freely. Flexible contact suited them best. And they didn't like step-parents appearing out of the ether; it was best if introductions to new partners were planned.

They got upset about unreliable or 'boring' conflict. They worried about the non-resident parent being 'alone'. They hated not being able to mention one parent to another. Children did best when they had a loving relationship with both parents. If the parents kept fighting, or using the children as pawns, or made a habit of talking down the other parent in front of them, it affected them and their long-term 'outcomes' very badly. So it was very important that parents avoided doing such things.

The above will strike the reader as a catalogue of utopian and unattainable expectations, but is included to illustrate that a great deal is known of ways in which children could be helped to survive the break-ups of their parents' marriages. Can policy-makers do anything to make the process by which parents handle family breakdown less damaging to children?'

What we need is a set of policies that serve the interests of all children, regardless of their parents' marital status. Among other things, they need to give proper support to divorcing couples so that they can continue to share the care of their children in an orderly and fruitful way. The new Family Mediation Service is a step in the right direction. Instead of aggravating the differences between divorcing parents, it provides the framework whereby divorcing parents can devise and agree upon the care arrangements that will underpin their new lives. There is no reason why these services could not be extended to offer the same help to parents after divorce, as they move on into those new lives and their children grow up.

As Beck and Beck-Gersheim point out, it is a social myth that marriage ends in divorce. 'Family research is only gradually waking up from its drowsy fixation on the nucleus of the family and discovering the other phenomenon of the "post-marital marriage", while still ignoring its opposite, "intrafamilial divorce". Like people who have lost an arm and still try to use it, divorced people live their marriages long after they have separation, with the ex still 'occupying as much mental space' as she or he did before.

Equating divorce with the break-up of a family, they say, is 'a partisan view describing the adults' wishes'. People who talk about broken families fail utterly to take into account the viewpoint of the children in those families. Marriages can be 'cancelled and remade' but families cannot; 'they live on in the persons of the children who move quietly across the boundaries of new partnerships and families'. As parents remarry, take on stepchildren, and have new children of their own, the original children's positions within these households are subject to constant change, to the point where the English language ceases to have words to describe many of the relationships. Divorce, say Beck and Beck-Gersheim, severs the links between social, legal and biological parenthood in much the same way as reproductive medicine.

The result, they say, is a world in which there is not much individualism. People may leave marriages 'to be free', but once they recouple they can find themselves part of 'whole networks of interrelated extended families'. These structures might be very hard to see from the outside, but it is essential that we understand them. When policy makers ignore them, and see the new social order solely in terms of marriage breakdown, they legislate for a world that does not exist outside the Office of Statistics.

'It takes quite a lot of empirically fortified wishful thinking,' Beck and Beck-Gersheim say, 'to overlook the upheavals in family and social structures being brought about by millions of divorces. Family research which continues to think in terms of nuclear families and suggests by amassing data on them that they are not subject to change will someday find itself on the shelf beside the other curious products of blind empiricism.'[35]

Family research, in other words, is blinkered by its own moral assumptions. The marriage renewal movement is blinkered in much the same way. It cannot see modern family structures for what they are because it does not want to see them. It can marshal plenty of facts to support its view that families living outside traditional marriage do a less than satisfactory job of rearing children. But instead of reaching out to help them, it promotes laws that will disadvantage them even further. How can that be fair?

The damaged child

Why did eight-year-old Marie Bentham go into her bedroom and hang herself with a skipping-rope? It was the last day of the Christmas break and just before she killed herself she had expressed fear about returning to school, where she'd been bullied the previous term. When her mother had complained about it, the school had looked into it and found that there had been a falling out between two groups of girls – awful, painful, but not at all unusual, and not usually a cause for grave concern.[36]

As it turned out, bullying was not the only problem Marie was grappling with. Her father had died two years earlier, very suddenly, of a heart attack, and his death had hit everyone in the family very hard. Friends and relatives told the press that Marie had withdrawn into herself afterwards. That, said a relation who would not be named, was when the bullying began.

Marie's last conversation with her mother went something like this: Marie said she didn't want to go back to school. Her mother said she had to. Marie protested. Her mother said, 'Go and get in bed, you've got to go to school.' As she left for her bedroom, Marie said, 'I hate you. I want my dad.' That was 8.30. Her mother went in to check on her at 10.30 and found her on the floor with the rope around her neck. Not everyone is sure that it was suicide. One aunt was certain it was a 'tragic accident'. But it is hard to hear the details without wondering what could and should have been done to prevent it.

Begin with the bullying question. 'It is very common,' anti-bullying officer Andrew Mellor told the *Daily Mail*, 'for children to be bullied around the time of a bereavement. We think it is due to changed reactions of other children who bully out of fear.' Not all children learn to cope with it, or know how and when to call for help. What's 'part of growing up' for one child is another child's scar for life. Marie Bentham may be the 'youngest bullying victim to take her own life', says Valerie Howarth of Childline, but she is hardly the youngest to have expressed suicidal tendencies. 'We have very young children ringing us up to say they are bullied and it is often verbal rather than physical abuse. Parents think it is something children have to put up with but it is wrong. Verbal abuse can break people's hearts.'[37]

In a world of happy, stable households, children whose hearts are broken on the playground can at least go home to parents who love them, who are finely attuned to them, who pick up on the earliest signs of distress. These serene and perfectly balanced parents are thus able to keep little problems of growing up from turning into the kind of big problems that scar children for life. If Marie's mother did not pick up on those signals, it may have been because she was bereaved. What sort of help was *she* getting? How did she manage to keep the family housed and fed after the sudden loss of her partner? How many of her problems were emotional? How many were material? How much did these problems preoccupy her, and take away from time she might have otherwise spent being 'attuned' to signs of distress from her children? Did she underestimate the distress her daughters were feeling, or did she over-compensate to make up for their loss?

What kind of support is on offer for mothers and fathers who are worried about a child who develops a stutter, or begins to withdraw into herself, or has nightmares, or seems anxious about everything, or stops sleeping, stops eating, bursts into tears at the slightest provocation, seems chronically fatigued and numb to the world around her? It depends on where you live, and most particularly on what sort of attitude your GP has to mental health. Phillip Graham, co-author of a book for parents on child depression sponsored by the Royal College of Psychiatry, says that while there are more and more GPs out there who are enlightened about the mental health needs of children, there are many more who will give you a lecture about pulling your socks up. This is often the only thing you can do, anyway, because the services you might imagine as helping a child in distress are just not there.[38] Even if you're 'lucky' and get referred to your local child and adolescent clinic, you will often have a long wait before being given an appointment. Some schools do go out of their way to give support in the interim, but many others will dismiss or obstruct your efforts – and here we run into another nightmare. There are at least two and often three different government agencies overseeing your child's progress by now – the NHS, the Department of Education, and Social Services. They do not speak the same language; they have conflicting aims, methods and areas of interest. And their statutory obligations clash.

If policy makers looked at their policies from the child's point of view, they would be able to see this problem immediately. But they don't, and so they can't. 'Laws affecting children,' says Anne McGillivray, 'are a bundle of opposing ideologies rarely centred on the needs of the child.'[39] They tell you more about the conflicting ways in which different sectors of society define childhood than about what children need or say they want.

Their areas of agreement are, if anything, even more revealing. According to Peter Wilson of the children's charity Young Minds, our own society's wilful blindness to children's mental health problems comes from our desire to see childhood as a time of perfect happiness. A child in distress stands in contradiction to that ideal picture: to take his problems seriously is to admit that the picture is false. But of course children suffer. 'Children go through the whole range of life's experiences. They lose things that matter to them – homes, schools parents, friends, pets . . . Can you believe it? Children actually have feelings!'[40]

Even fifteen years ago, the standard line on child depression was that it didn't exist. Now we've gone to the other extreme. The latest government figures suggest that one in five children suffers from mental health problems at any given time, and that half of all children will do so at some point before they turn eighteen. The figures are highest for adolescents, but it's now accepted that at least 2 per cent of children under twelve suffer from clinical depression, with another

4–5 per cent in that same age group 'showing significant distress'.[41] This is a sharp rise from fifteen years ago, when the boldest estimates put the rate of depression amongst children at 0.1 per cent. Not everyone in the mental health world sees these figures as signalling an epidemic. The very term 'depression' is open to question. Many therapists shy away from blanket labels, and prefer to talk about depressive symptoms which will manifest themselves to differing degrees in different people, and for a wide variety of reasons. So, as author and psychoanalyst Darian Leader puts it, a rise in the number of people being diagnosed as suffering from depression tells you a little about the patients themselves and quite a lot about the doctor making the diagnosis.[42] If we've gone from a 0.1 per cent child depression rate to 6 or 7 per cent rate, it must be at least partly due to the fact that the mental health fraternity did not even acknowledge it existed fifteen years ago, and now seems ready to see it as endemic.

If the powers that be now accept that one in five children is suffering from mental health problems, it is partly due to a concerted effort on the part of many charities and professional organisations to make them take children seriously. But it's also due to the fact that these same groups and organisations have vastly expanded their terms. The Mental Health Foundation's Bright Futures initiative is a case in point. It is probably the most ambitious child-centred project ever seen in this country. During a three-year inquiry, it gathered up over a thousand pieces of written evidence from professionals as well as oral testimony from health workers, teachers, service providers, academics, parents and children. Its central aim is to come up with a 'holistic' way of addressing children's emotional difficulties. Such a system would provide swift and non-stigmatised help for children with major problems, but at the same time it would aim to prevent most children from suffering serious distress by catching problems before they became too severe. At the same time it would seek not to pathologise children with problems, or isolate them from their families and peers. Instead it would aim to help them as informally as possible in everyday settings. It would encourage children to find their own solutions where possible, but also provide prompt support when necessary. Instead of focusing on the negative, the main objective would be to promote 'emotional well-being'. This too is an infinitely expandable term, because an environment that fosters well-being in children, like an environment that respects their rights, is a world in which children are protected from war, famine, poverty, homelessness and all other deprivation, not to mention violence, abuse and all other forms of cruelty.

So to campaign for emotional well-being is sometimes to enlist in a programme for social justice so far-reaching that even Marx would gasp at the thought of it. But the polite term for it is positive mental health, and the key concept in positive mental health is 'early intervention'. There have been early intervention programmes in the US for more than twenty years, studies of which suggest that by helping troubled children early, you can decrease the likelihood of their developing into 'more serious and troubling behaviours and problems' in adolescence. There has been a huge increase in such programmes in this country over the past decade – many of them borrowed whole from US projects, while others are home grown. They range from the very loose to the very structured, the locally defined to the generic, the voluntary to the virtually mandatory. Some focus exclusively on children, while others seek to improve the quality of their home lives by focusing on their parents.

The good ones work with parents rather than against them. To give an idea of what this means in practice, consider the programme that Jane Whittington pioneered at Westwood

Park Primary School in Guildford.[43] The idea behind it was a presumed link between her pupils' fear of failure and 'what we saw at the school gates'. It was not uncommon for a mother to nod to a child without even saying hello, and for that child to wordlessly follow her home. 'And sometimes there was artwork that the children had put a great deal of effort into, that the mothers binned before they left the playground.'

Instead of taking the easy way out, and dismissing them as bad mothers, she decided to think of them as mothers in distress. She thought that if they could find a way of giving them some support, they might have the space and the energy to give more to their children. And so now there was a family worker in the school to whom parents can turn when they need assistance. There are also parenting classes that are proving very popular. The title of one series was 'How Small Changes Can Make Big Differences'. Example: if you have just had a second child, and your firstborn is acting up, you can solve the problem almost overnight just by making sure you spend half an hour alone with that child every evening.

There is no pressure on parents to join these classes. According to the Parenting Education and Support Forum – an umbrella organisation for the rapidly expanding parenting education movement – classes just don't work unless they're defined locally, relevant to those local parents' needs, and *voluntary*.[44] A successful intervention programme, says Sheila Hegarty, is rooted in respect. By this she means respect for the child, for the parent, and for the many difficulties that a child and a parent have to negotiate in life. Hegarty works in North London with a project run by Elfrida Rathbone called Parent and Co. 'Our ethos is very much coming from the understanding that parenting is difficult for everyone, that parents know best, and that both parents and children are important.' Parent and Co tries to break the cycle by working with parents and children in the home, by setting up informal discussion groups, and running intensive ten-week courses that get parents to look more closely at the way they relate to their children. In all instances, it's the parents who set the agenda. There's an atmosphere of trust because 'we listen to parents rather than issuing advice. We never say we have all the answers.' The hope is that if they give the parents the confidence to tap into their own intuitive knowledge of children and child-rearing, they will come up with a much better strategy that an outside expert could ever have imagined.[45]

This, then, is the parenting education movement's idea of 'best practice'. As such, it is very much in line with ideas of 'best practice' promulgated by the children's mental health movement, and by the broader campaign for emotional literacy with which both are associated. At its very, very best, it's an approach that is sensitive to context. It respects the parent without occluding the child, and the child without occluding the parent. It values the autonomy of children while also protecting them, takes their problems seriously without labelling them. It focuses on emotional wellbeing without neglecting material circumstances. Most important, it posits children and counsellors, parents and 'educators' as equals.

There are no experts issuing context-blind edicts from on high. Family life is problematic, but not hopeless. Solutions are pragmatic, not moral. It's understood that while we live in difficult times, they are not entirely corrupt times. Some things have become easier for parents and children, while others have got worse. Once you know where the problem areas are, you can do something about them. As the *Bright Futures* report suggests, you can devise policies that alleviate the stresses which tax all parents and make the vulnerable ones go off the deep end. And by 'decreasing exposure to adverse life events (such as the impact of parental alcoholism, mental illness or divorce) . . . or increasing the number of protective factors (communication and problem solving skills, or sources of emotional support)' you can make it more likely that a child will learn how to be 'resilient, to thrive despite adversity'.[46]

When *Bright Futures* was published, it got a positive and approving reception. The consensus was that anything we could do to 'improve the odds' for children was something worth doing. There was a good deal of sentimental talk, too, about children being the 'nation's future'. But the problem with children is that they turn into teenagers.

Teenage mutants

'Imagine you are fourteen years old,' says the leader in the *Guardian* on 1 May 1998. 'You are living in a seaside town. Your mother has a partner who is not your father but is devoted to you and your mother . . . Then suddenly and violently this whole world collapses. Your home is besieged by tabloid reporters knocking at the door. They camp out in their cars right outside your house, causing confusion, bemusement, disorientation. In the middle of the night the police arrive, and for your own and your mother's safety take both of you to a safe house for fear of vigilante groups as well as the tabloid mafia. You face a dreadful future. It looks as though you will have to leave your home, your school, your neighbourhood. Much, much worse, your mother's identity is suddenly destroyed. She is not who you thought she was. She has a notorious past . . .'[47]

This piece about the plight of Mary Bell's daughter is a rare piece of empathetic journalism. It's rare, too, in that it extends empathy to a teenager. But perhaps I should rephrase that. Mary's daughter is not the only teenager to be described warmly in recent press history, but she belongs to another of those clubs you can only join by virtue of a terrible tragedy. Thus, the *Daily Mail* suspends its usual disapproval of teenage mothers when telling the sad story of a fourteen-year-old whose newborn baby's father had committed suicide after being told he could not visit the house. Teenagers who die while canoeing for a Duke of Edinburgh Award, or when their bus goes off the road into a ravine on a school trip, are described as joys and vibrant members of their communities who will never be forgotten and can never be replaced. But while they live, their public profile is a lot less favourable.

A much-publicised recent study found that almost one in every hundred 13–15-year-old girls in the UK becomes pregnant. But it's hard to find an article about a girl in that age range who *isn't* pregnant. News-breaking teen pregnancy stories from 1998 include:

1   A 12-year-old boy who was let off school to be at his baby's birth. The mother's parents said he was 'mature-looking'; after the news of the pregnancy broke, he told the press that he'd been shocked at first but was all right about it now, and wanted 'to be there for the baby and to be part of it all'. The mother was 15.[48]

2   A 12-year-old girl from Poole, Dorset, who gave birth to a 7lb 4oz daughter that was fathered by a 13-year-old boy. She didn't realise she was pregnant until a week before the birth, when she complained to her mother that she was suffering from stomach pains.[49]

3   A 16-year-old boy who went to lawyers to fight for access to his 3-month-old son, whom he had hardly seen despite the fact that the mother, also 16, lived next door. It seems they broke up during the pregnancy. The

mother, who was waiting for her exam results, told the press that she 'couldn't bear the thought of him seeing Ryan again, never mind getting custody. If there's even the slightest chance that he's getting anywhere near Ryan, I'll move away and no one will know where I've gone . . . Christopher was meant to help out financially, but all I've ever had from his family is two second-hand baby-gros, three pairs of socks and a Moses basket. When Ryan was three weeks old, at Easter, they sent a 99p chocolate bunny. As if a baby that age could have chocolate.'[50]

4   A woman who becomes a grandmother at 29 after her 14-year-old daughter gives birth to a son. 'It's amazing how history has repeated itself, but I could have killed Gemma when I found out she was pregnant. I know more than anyone how hard it is to bring up a baby at that age.' When it happened to her, she told reporters, she was still living at home with her parents too, just like Gemma, 'and they were fuming. They were so ashamed.'[51]

5   A divorcee and single mother, also of Poole, Dorset, who discovered that her 15- and 16-year-old daughters were pregnant on the same day. She'd put both on the pill when they turned 14. But 'children grow up so fast these days. Unfortunately my girls sometimes forgot to take it, which is why we're in this mess. What has happened to me could have happened to any number of families with girls their age.' Her older daughter knew the father was her boyfriend, but the younger one had had casual sex with two 18-year-olds and so wasn't sure. Although there was to be a DNA test after the birth, this girl was very upset that she didn't know who the father was and had

been crying herself to sleep, her mother said. Struggling to look on the bright side, the mother added that, 'At least she knows I'll always be there. I'm still young enough to be able to bring up babies so she can go back to school afterwards, get her exams and make a life for herself. I'll be the child's legal guardian until Miranda is 16 and I'll happily continue looking after the baby when she goes to work.' Despite these words of generosity, the *Daily Mail* still sees fit to point out that, 'Interestingly, Mrs Way's daughters have followed in her footsteps. Three-times-married Mrs Way, 34, has had four children by three different fathers and had an abortion at 14. She fell pregnant with Charlene while she was still in her teens.' Their story, says the headline, 'speaks volumes about the family today'.[52]

Their story got picked up by most papers because it happened to break in the same week as the government released depressing new figures showing an 11 per cent rise in under-age pregnancies in one year. Three-quarters of these were fifteen, and half of them had abortions. The new figures also confirmed that Britain's overall teenage pregnancy rate was twice that of Germany, four times that of France and seven times that of the Netherlands. Changing the direction of the trend would be a difficult job, Tessa Jowell (the Minister for Health) told the press, because it was so closely linked with so many social factors. The sort of girls most likely to become pregnant very early had low educational attainment, suffered from emotional problems, and had mothers who had been teenage mothers themselves. The Social Exclusion Unit was finding a 'common thread running through all its projects, whether teenage pregnancies, sleeping rough, deprived neighbourhoods or school exclusions', and this was 'young people from poor areas with no jobs, no training, who left school completely unequipped for adult life. They are in danger of ending up homeless, becoming pregnant too early and staying on benefit too long.'[53]

Although the government has been careful not to imply that they are poor *because* they're pregnant, the official line on the teenage pregnancy problem is tilted in such a way that you could easily assume that they will be rescued from poverty if they can be persuaded not to become pregnant. Hence all that is said about identifying the problem before it happens, and putting schoolgirls who fit the high-risk profile on to 'baby danger' lists, so that they can have the extra attention and encouragement that could keep them away from 'premature parenthood'.[54]

In spite of all the talk about the many forms of deprivation these girls have suffered, the government has still been keen to stress that teenage pregnancy points to a moral sickness in our society. Tony Blair's much discussed comments on the two pregnant 12-year-olds who hit the news at the end of the summer of 1999 were very much in this vein. He was 'appalled' that it could have come to this. But even if you agree that it is a terrible shame for a 12-year-old to be having sex at all – it is still important to put these tragedies in context. As the Family Policy Studies Centre points out in its briefing paper on the Social Exclusion Unit's report, there is not a new epidemic of teenage pregnancy. Rates of conception amongst under-20s have remained more or less constant in the UK since the early 1980s, and only a tiny number of them are aged twelve. Although the UK does have the highest rate of teenage births in Western Europe, the decline in the rate of births in other countries is not a reflection of lower conception rates but higher rates of abortion. So why the sudden interest in the problem of teenage pregnancy? The FPSC suggests that it has become a moral problem for the nation because it is a fiscal problem for the government. These teenage mothers cost money to maintain. But to remedy the larger structural problems that cause high rates of teenage pregnancy – their lack of training and job opportunities – would cost even more. This implies that, by turning teenage pregnancy into a moral problem, it can look as if it's doing something even as it fails to address the roots of the problem.[55]

And there is another problem – the new war on teenage pregnancy does not sit comfortably with other policy initiatives directed towards young men. To imply that these girls will really be able to improve themselves just by deferring motherhood is to undermine the standard explanations for the other big 'youth' problem – disaffected, disconnected young men. Just about the only risk these young men *don't* run is that of falling pregnant. And yet they're still not able to pull themselves together. So what's holding them back? What is the source of their distress? Why, for example, is the suicide rate for adolescent males five times what it is for adolescent females, and why did the suicide rate for men aged between 15 and 24 rise by 85 per cent between 1980 and 1990?[56] Over the past decade we've heard many explanations for the rise and rise of distressed and disaffected youth. It's unemployment, some say; it's the dearth of good role models, say others. It's sour grapes at the sight of girls doing so well in school and in jobs; the erosion of the rites of passage that once ushered their fathers and grandfathers into adulthood; the erosion of marriage; the disappearance of the job for life. It's drugs, poor schooling, inadequate government support for those who are forced to leave home at 16. It's popular culture. It's different things to different young men in different classes. It's everything, so it should come as no surprise to hear that it's not unique to Britain.

A 1998 report by the Work-Life research centre based on in-depth interviews with 18–30-year-olds in Britain, Ireland, Norway, Portugal and Sweden revealed that this age group felt

trapped in a 'protracted limbo'. This was often due to the
added time many had to spend in training. Although they
knew training was a good investment, it did mean that they
remained economically dependent on their parents, on the
state, or on student loans. And although most of them did
speak of wanting to settle down at some point, talk of settling
down had a quality of unreality for them. First of all, there
was the insecurity of the job market. The best way to cope
with this was to stay on one's toes and live in a sort of
'extended present'. But this made the prospect of settling
down and planning for a family seem all the more bizarre.
'Few young people have caring commitments and many find
it difficult to anticipate these.' Another less polite way to put
this is to say that they live in a society that gives them fewer
and fewer good reasons to 'grow up'.[57]

A study from 1995 that also drew upon in-depth interviews with young people, this time in Scotland, suggests
that it has become harder than ever for them to make the
transition from dependence to independence. Because it's
so much harder to enter the labour market, and because
most jobs require so much more training, many cannot
afford the basic props of adult life at 16, 18 or even 25, and
so they go through a prolonged period of 'semi-independ-
ence'. Even if they are in work, they can rarely command
adult-level salaries. Those who are dependent on the state
will not qualify for many adult-level benefits: the level of
government support for young people has been massively
reduced since the early 1980s. The result is that young
people trying to get up on their own feet must depend much
more on their families than they (or their parents) ever
expected. This new pressure on family support systems
comes at a time when relations between the two generations will be very strained already. Young people who want
to have independent lives will find it difficult to remain

dependent; parents who provide the support will resent their children's resentment. The law is unclear about what the various parties have a right to demand and expect. 'Where family support is concerned, the initiative lies with the giver, who retains the power to provide or withhold support, rather than with the potential receiver, who may find it difficult to ask.'[58] As another study put it, 'claiming rights is definitely not seen as a legitimate part of family life. Even where one person accepts a responsibility to help, the other does not have the right to claim, or even to expect, assistance.'[59]

How an individual family manages this uncharted territory has a huge effect on their young adult children's chances in life. Even where parents have good relationships with their children and live in stable households, with plenty of money put aside for those little surprises in life, this transition period can be fraught with conflict. And if the parents' own marriage is in trouble, if they are in financial difficulty, if there is a stepparent who feels less inclined to put up with the problems of not quite grown children, if that young person is not in his parents' view paying enough board, or appears to be living the life of Riley, then the chances of that young person not getting family support only stand to increase – as do the odds of that person falling into extreme poverty and/or homelessness.

Neither this nor the previous study got the tabloid treatment, nor did they excite much comment in the quality press. This is partly to do with the fact that it lacked a sensational hook. A joyrider or a 12-year-old mother can give a human face to a problem; next to such stories, a survey of young people reflecting thoughtfully on life, work and the future doesn't have a chance. But the main reason they sank out of sight so fast is that they did not illustrate the 'youth problem' as our popular culture currently portrays it. The youth stories that excite mass interest are invariably those which suggest they have too much freedom and too few restraints, and are spiralling out of control.

This would explain the strange reception accorded to stories of exam success. Wherever there are reports of good results, there are other reports claiming that they're not worth quite as much as people claim, or that one person's success is another person's disaster. Thus, better results for girls in SATS, GCSEs, A-levels or university degrees mean that their male classmates are doing less well. At the same time, girls who do well in school are thought perhaps to be doing themselves great harm in the process. They are pushing themselves too hard; they're in danger of becoming anorexics. Or if they're still eating, they're failing to balance their diets and developing some very unhealthy habits, and so earning headlines like 'Child Drinkers Double Intake in Seven Years',[60] 'Dead at Just 13: The Drugs Girl Whose Parents Gave Her Everything',[61] or 'Youngsters Who are Hooked on Deadly Lifestyle: perils of a generation who drink too much, eat all the wrong food and don't take enough exercise'.[62]

Poverty, whenever it is mentioned, gets treated like just another appalling addiction, as in this discussion of a study of young people on inner city estates:

> About 100,000 young people between the ages of 16 and 24 now occupy the position in society that sociologists call Status Zero. It describes those who are not in education, training or employment and have effectively dropped out of society. They are, in short, the bedrock of what has come to be known as the underclass. 'Aimlessly drifting, with no apparent purpose in life, no sense of attachment to mainstream society, with ever-diminishing prospects of employment, and likely to be involved in criminal activity,' that is how they are described in *The Drop Out Society*, a report published yesterday by the

National Youth Agency . . . It concluded that much of
what society takes for granted – education, qualifications, training, work, career prospects, a secure income –
is 'irrelevant to the realities that drive and control
them' . . . Two questions arise: What happens to the
children before they are three? And why does 12 years of
schooling do nothing to compensate for it?[63]

Why would anyone expect *any* amount of schooling to make
poverty go away? Some people do ask this question, but never
with quite as much energy as those who use badly-behaving
youths as proof that schools have been used too long as
'agents of social engineering' rather than in their 'proper role
of implanting discipline, knowledge, and skills'.[64] When dia-
tribes against underclass youths do take their environment
into account, it is to highlight its depravity. Theodore
Dalrymple's account is typical of this sort of New
Victorianism:

. . . the world of the British underclass is utterly charm-
less and without any redeeming features whatsoever. It
has not even the bonhomie which is noticeable in some
societies during hard times. It is a world of the routine
neglect of children, of violence, crime, illiteracy, unemployment, illegitimacy, addiction, drunkenness and
prostitution. It is a Hobbesian world in which no one
owes any allegiance to anyone else, except in defiance of
the law and the police. Even parents have scant loyalty
to their children, and frequently cast them out as soon as
they have become a burden on finances.[65]

That was in the *Daily Telegraph*, but the same themes figure in
New Labour's approach to under-achieving boys. Very important ministers have called them 'our worst social problem',

and have expressed alarm at the growth of a 'boys behaving badly culture' and police figures showing that 'much street crime in London is carried out by schoolboy truants, many of whom cannot write their names or tell the time'. They've also expressed concern about the conviction amongst such boys that only 'cissies' do well in school. With the best of intentions, but no firm evidence, they have linked this attitude to the lack of male role models in schools. Also mindful of the fact that 'men have traditionally been deterred from working in primary schools by low pay', they have discussed the possibility of introducing a new category of 'super-teachers' (male teachers?) on an 'enhanced pay scale',[66] and also providing them with adult 'mentors' to advise on careers, relationships and drugs.[67]

But these well-meaning proposals look very pale next to our Frankensteinian image of 'Youth Gone Wrong'. The fact that this is based on myth and an economical use of the truth does nothing to diminish its power. Bad teenagers in the public eye exist primarily to bear witness to the bad parents and bad schools that failed them. In politics, they serve to personify moral decay, and justify calls for a new morality.

4

The New Morality

The four cornerstones of the new morality

Selfish parents in non-traditional families raise damaged children, who become antisocial teenagers who go on to erode the fabric of our society. This is the story of modern family life as told by the social conservatives who have dominated the family debate over the past two decades. A few see free-market capitalism as the prime agent of social decay, but most blame feminism, the liberalisation of divorce laws and the subsidising of 'immoral life styles' by the welfare state.

Until very recently, anyone who held parents responsible for the erosion of society was by definition right-wing – and was, according to his left-wing critics, 'blaming the victim'. But over the past ten years, the 'vicious culture argument' has been seeping slowly but steadily over to the other side. It's easy to see how: it sits comfortably with the 'vicious cycle argument' that dominates the left-of-centre debates on child neglect, child abuse, teenage pregnancy, domestic violence, juvenile delinquency, addiction, and even unemployment.

The scandals and panics we have been considering in this book have fed and fuelled both lines of argument. If you line them up, it is also clear that they have gone a long way to convincing most people in this country that 'the family' is in crisis and needs urgent correction. Together, these scandals have convinced most people that there's something deeply wrong about the way we run our society, and something very important missing in our political understanding of it. The race to name that missing something has yet to be decided, but the word that comes up most frequently is morality.

In this, the final section of the book, I mean to show how politicians have engaged with the morality question over the past five years, and how they have modernised it. I'll move on to indicate how New Labour has sought to explain its new ideas to the general public, and how it has translated them into policy. I'll then say what I think of these policies – what's good about them, what's worrying and what's missing. Finally, I'll explain how I think the policies should change, and why I believe ordinary parents should be taking part in this redrafting exercise. My main objection to the new morality as framed by politicians today is that it is a top-down exercise, to be imposed by wise leaders on a population of parents who do not know what's for their own good. My own view is that parents with consciences know much more than most politicians about the practical and ethical problems of modern family life: any new morality should take this pool of knowledge into account. A government that was humble enough to tap into their resources would, I believe, have a chance of resolving at least some of the terrible problems we've been looking at in this book.

Moral lessons for a nation

In a secular, individualist, free market age, it takes a very large tragedy for an entire nation to rise up in disgust at the way we are now and cry out as one for moral rearmament. In this country, it took the death of the inner-city headmaster, Phillip Lawrence.

His killer was a 15-year-old boy named Learco Chindamo.[1] He was half Italian and half Filipino, and lived with his mother and stepfather in a sink estate in Camden. A failure at school, his main interests seem to have been truanting, martial arts and drugs. He belonged to a gang that modelled itself somewhat amateurishly on the triads. On the afternoon of 8 December 1995, this gang decided to settle a dispute with a 13-year-old pupil at St George's, a Roman Catholic secondary school in Maida Vale. They turned up at the gates just as school was coming out and went to work on the boy with an iron bar. They did not realise they were carrying out their attack in full view of the headmaster.

From the moment he had arrived three years earlier, Philip Lawrence had taken a strong, unbending and much-admired stand on violence and antisocial behaviour. To make his point, he had had to expel more than 60 pupils. It was, he believed, because he had succeeded in changing the school ethos that the school's exam successes had risen by 16 per cent in one year. His behaviour policy had proved popular with parents. The roll had gone up by 47 per cent. 'I am giving parents what they want; Christian values in their children,' he told a local newspaper. 'We believe that there is a difference between right and wrong. There is no relativist position. There is forgiveness, but there is wrong. And that is something that parents of whatever religious background are buying into. It's what their children need.'[2]

He was aware of the fact that the world beyond the school

gates was still full of dangers for his pupils, which is one of the reasons why he was in the habit of watching over them as they left school at the end of the day. And so it was that he caught Learco and his friends in action. When he ran to rescue his pupil, they abandoned the 13-year-old boy and fled, but Philip Lawrence kept chasing them. According to eyewitness reports, Lawrence soon caught up with Learco and tried to stop him by putting his hand on his shoulder. And then, as a crowd of mostly children looked on, Learco kicked and slapped Lawrence before stabbing him in the chest.

Lawrence was able to stagger back inside, but then he collapsed. After open-heart surgery on the school floor, and six hours in the operating theatre, he died.[3] There was an immediate nationwide uproar – and well there should have been. But before we take a look at the saturation coverage, I'd like you to put your minds back to a not entirely different outrage a year earlier, in 1994, in which another man named Lawrence was also killed on the street by thugs. Actually, there were two very important differences between these stories. In the case of Philip Lawrence, the victim was white, the perpetrators foreign and/or black. In the case of Steven Lawrence, it was the other way around – the victim who was black and the attackers who were white. In the view of his parents, this was why there was no coverage of his murder in the papers the next day. In the public eye, his mother said, his life had less value than it would have done had he been white.

It would take a five-year campaign by Steven's family and an official inquiry before the public could see the larger injustices at work in the police bungling of his case. But in the case of the Philip Lawrence murder, the public needed no prompting. The news of this headmaster's 'death in the line of duty' seemed emblematic of all that was wrong with cities, schools, families, teenagers, undesirable aliens and the underclass, and so the public response was huge and immediate. And it went on for some time.

On Saturday we heard of Philip Lawrence's 'bold vision' for his 'troubled' school.[4] On Monday we read of the courage of his widow, Frances Lawrence, as she struggled to give her four children, aged between 21 and 8, a 'normal Christmas'. On Monday, we also heard about the anger in the community. At Sacred Heart Church in Kilburn, three teenage girls went to mass with 'linked arms, their eyes reddened with crying'. Twelve-year-old Oswald Smith talked to reporters about how much he had loved St George's, 'but now it will never be the same again'. A second child told reporters it was 'like a video nasty coming to life'.[5] In his sermon, Father Matthew O'Shea talked of their collective horror at the sudden way 'the terrible things they read about in newspapers had come closer to home'.

In this speech, as elsewhere, poverty is not the central issue. There is the occasional allusion to 'sink estates' and 'mean streets', but these are generally subsumed under the category 'senseless evil'. 'How can you even begin to understand the senseless death of a good man?' is how Father O'Shea put it in his sermon that Sunday. Writing in the parish newsletter, Father Ray Warren, a governor of the school, blamed Lawrence's death on 'the evil that exists in our society'.

Meanwhile, bouquets from children and parents piled up outside the school gates. Susan Lake, secretary of the local branch of the Union of Catholic Mothers, called the stabbing 'premeditated' and 'unforgivable'.[6] On the same day we read about all this, we also read the letter the youngest Lawrence child wrote after his father's death, asking Father Christmas to give him back his father.[7]

Then we heard about the open letter Frances Lawrence had sent to the pupils at St George's, in which she urged them to learn from her husband's death. 'Violence is not a knife in the hand. It grows, like a poison tree, inside people who, unlike yourselves, have not learnt to value other human beings.' The way forward, she said, was 'to create a world in which goodness is never again destroyed by evil'.

The Prime Minister echoed these sentiments when he spoke of his own grief. He went on to highlight the efforts that were already under way to address 'the whole range of issues covering the safety of staff and pupils in our schools'. By now, leader writers had begun to call on Parliament to come up with some 'hard-edged administrative measures' to deal with out-of-control inner city teenage boys. 'There is no doubt that too many of our urban streets are insecure; that the perpetrators of violence are often disconcertingly young, that many of our young of school-going age live lives of little parental or institutional control. There should be no doubt, also, that the problem can be solved only in part by tougher laws and tougher policing. Yet the lawmakers' attention must focus afresh on the knife, the weapon which sent Mr Lawrence to his death.'[8]

That Sunday, Frances Lawrence added new weight to this suggestion with an 'impassioned plea' for the government to clamp down on the carrying of knives. Britain could no longer sustain a 'lily-livered approach to violence. We have to tackle it head-on and find the root causes. It may take some courage but that is the only route forward.' She commended her husband as an example. 'Like St George, he knew there were dragons out there but he felt you must confront them, otherwise those dragons would perpetuate.' On another, colder day, her metaphors might have seemed over-emotional; but on that day, they matched the public mood perfectly. When she asked the nation to learn from his death, the nation listened.[9]

It was still listening the following October when Learco

Chindamo was convicted for the murder of her husband, and for causing grievous bodily harm to the 13-year-old boy he had gone to St George's to attack.[10] Shortly after the judge ordered that he be 'detained indefinitely', Frances issued a manifesto calling for a national debate on what Philip Johnston referred to as 'the question that politicians are often reluctant to confront: morality'.

Frances was determined, she said, that something good should come out of 'the terrible violence that pierced the heart of my family'. The roots of this violence were indiscipline, amorality, and family breakdown. What was needed, she said, was 'a new ethos'. 'There is a yearning for action to restore a moral code to the centre of our national life. This is not nostalgia; it is an honest recognition that we are in danger of losing sight of the fundamentals.'

The manifesto received a thoughtful and respectful press. According to Philip Johnston, this was a good sign in and of itself. The British, he said, were 'temperamentally uncomfortable with crusades and moral rearmament movements. Yet faced with the pain and courage of Mrs Lawrence, politicians of all parties have responded to a popular clamour for a reassertion of the values that appear to have been abandoned.' Referring to the Belgian paedophile scandal, which was also in the headlines that week, he went on to say that just as 'ghastly events in Belgium triggered a crisis of morality that last weekend brought thousands on to the streets in protest, so Mrs Lawrence has struck a chord in Britain that has resonated across the land'.

In a sense, he continued, she was 'pushing at an open door'. The 'rights politics' of the 1960s and 1970s had been badly discredited, and now even Tony Blair spoke from a 'strong religious standpoint'. Conservative thinkers, of course, 'had for years sought to inject a moral dimension into policy debate, often to the derision of their opponents and commentators. Mrs Thatcher's Victorian values, John Major's "Back to Basics" and John Redwood's utterances on single parenthood have all foundered on the rocks of ridicule. Douglas Hurd's efforts to provoke discussion on the "civic society" met with indifference.' But 'Mrs Lawrence's intervention has given the politicians a chance to embrace morality without it being seen purely as cynical opportunism'. She had 'issued a challenge not only to the nation's political leaders, but to all its citizens. She has asked for nothing less than a change in behaviour and attitudes'.[11]

And so the debate widened. That same week, the government announced an initiative to 'promote the moral development of pupils in schools'. There were promises that moral lessons emphasising 'the value of families, the law, justice and "the common good of society" could be incorporated into the National Curriculum in two years' time. The following week, amid reports of politicians of all persuasions madly outbidding each other in response to Mrs Lawrence, there was much discussion of a report showing the long-neglected but suddenly newsworthy decline of institutions – such as the Church, the Scout movement, and voluntary groups like the Round Table and the Women's Institutes – that once were able to do such a good job of encouraging civic responsibility. 'Events like the murder of Philip Lawrence have focused attention on the ways in which civil society and informal social networks have collapsed,' said Barry Knight, secretary of the newly formed Foundation for a Civil Society. 'People's lack of civil involvement has gone hand in hand with a growing sense of their powerlessless.'[12]

But he spoke too soon, because within the week government ministers had responded to the 'mood of considerable public concern' that had been 'given voice' by Mrs Lawrence, by placing pressure on programme makers, distributors and censors to 'consider afresh the impact of screen violence on children'.[13]

A few weeks later, it was the anniversary of Philip Lawrence's murder and Jack Straw, Michael Howard and Cardinal Basil Hume were among those on hand to give support to little Lucien Lawrence as he unveiled a plaque to his father outside the gates of St George's. It was an emotional occasion; many of the children present were 'visibly upset'. Frances Lawrence worked hard to remind them that, even in death, their former headmaster could continue to be their inspiration. The plaque was above all for his former pupils, she said. 'In the early morning or at dusk as they walk through the school gates, perhaps they will pause for a while and consider the words on the plaque. They will visualise how he would stand at the gates and send them on their way cheerfully and remember that he cared deeply for each one of them; that he respected and delighted in each of his pupils' individuality and considered each one of them to be capable of greatness. They will remember that when times were tough he gave them hope and that he never let them down.'

After the unveiling of the plaque, it was Frances' turn to be praised. Michael Howard praised her for her courage in turning away from the 'barrenness of despair' and trying to make something positive come out of her husband's death. There was talk of the youth reward scheme he had set up in Lawrence's name, to encourage young people to stand up against lawlessness.[14]

For a while, there was even talk of Frances Lawrence herself entering politics. There were more reports of talks she'd had with Labour leaders, with Tory leaders, and finally with David Alton to discuss his idea for a new Christian Democrat Party. Then we heard that she had given her support to the non-partisan People's Trust, which was to campaign to clean up sleaze in Westminster and which was funded by none other than Mohammed Al-Fayed. She told the press that she had received many letters urging her to make sure her moral agenda stayed on the agenda by going into politics.[15]

But it was not to be – not in the 1997 election, anyway – and it was as the campaign got under way that she faded into the background. Either she stopped giving speeches, or the papers stopped reporting them. She ceased to be a symbol of moral regeneration. The school for which her husband died slid down the league tables once again, and returned to being a symbol of urban decay. But it was not the same story for the campaign she had started. The public continued to warm to the idea of a moral agenda. In the end, it fell to the other politician at the unveiling to take it to Westminster.

The crisis in modern family life had long been a concern for Jack Straw. By the beginning of 1996, he had a clear idea not just of what he thought was wrong but what he thought he might do to make it right. He drew many of his ideas from the political philosophy of the moment, communitarianism, a central idea of which is that children are failing because there is a 'parenting deficit'. In the original American version, parents are not parenting adequately because they are working too hard, divorcing too often, and are more interested in exercising their rights than in honouring their responsibilities. In the view of communitarian extraordinaire, Amitai Etzioni, they are able to do these things with impunity because they no longer get moral support from their communities. For moral support read friends and neighbours nudging and chiding each other for being too selfish, and too obsessed with rights, and urging them on to a more responsible, child-centred, civic path through use of 'gentle suasion'. And if that doesn't work, naming and shaming.

In its American form, communitarianism has faced strong

criticism from intellectuals. In spite of this, many of its key
terms became part of the political vocabulary during the early
and mid-1990s, not just in the US but in this country and
indeed all over Europe. Its main attraction to the Labour
modernisers is that it turned 'the vicious culture argument' on
its head. Instead of 'blaming the victims', it suggested that the
best way forward was to offer parents better guidance and
support. Instead of going on and on about bad parenting leading to moral decay, it looked forward to a day when a nation
of competent, civic-minded parents might be able to work
hand in hand with government to generate a new spirit of
moral renewal. The Labour election manifesto expressed this
vision very clearly. So did Jack Straw, Tony Blair and David
Blunkett in speech after speech. But it took another scandal
for the key idea to get across.

Straw and son

A 17-year-old boy goes into a South London pub with three
friends and chats up a woman. Or is it the other way round?
The woman is hoping to score some cannabis resin. The boy
offers to help her, and help her he does. But the woman turns
out to be Dawn Alford, investigative reporter for the *Mirror*,
who's come to this pub after receiving a tip-off from an anony-
mous caller. As she already knows, and as the rest of the
country is about to find out, the boy is the son of a cabinet
minister. When the scandal breaks on 24 December 1997,
the *Mirror* is not able to say *which* cabinet minister. But of
course everyone in the media business knows, and so all the
national papers have a great deal of fun ringing Jack Straw to
ask him what position he is taking on all this in his capacity
as Home Secretary.

During his few months in the cabinet, Straw has already

made his mark as an 'implacable' opponent of the legalisation
of soft drugs. He's introduced a series of initiatives aimed at
cracking down on youth crime, *and* the causes of youth
crime, one of which is – he has told us time and time again –
ineffectual parenting. He's well known for using homilies
from his own family whenever he discusses family policy, but
this time he can say very little. His son is still a minor and so,
under English law, he cannot be named. But the law is not the
same in Scotland, so Straw and Son are splashed all over the
front pages of the *Scotsman*, the *Scottish Daily Mail* and the
Daily Record. Their English editions do not include the item,
but *France Soir*, which also runs the story, does nothing to
prevent it from appearing on newsstands in Britain. It dis-
misses the episode as a typical example of British hypocrisy.[16]
But British politicians are calling it a French farce. By now, the
names are public knowledge in Ireland and Scotland – and
everywhere else, too, thanks to the Internet. Roger Gale, vice-
chairman of the Tory media sub-committee in the Commons,
tells reporters that, 'It is ludicrous that one part of the United
Kingdom, because of a quirk in the law, is unable to publish
the name that virtually everybody in public knows.'[17]

And so, on 2 January 1998, a High Court judge lifts the
ban. Minutes later, at a 'hastily arranged press conference',
Straw Senior is able to speak for the first time about 'his shock
and pain' upon discovering that his son had been accused of
dealing drugs. It seems that 17-year-old William was something of a newcomer to the counterculture. At Pimlico School,
Westminster, he was known as a 'swot'. He had already taken
a maths A-level, and was now doing A-levels in politics,
physics and religious studies. On Christmas Eve, the day the
story broke in the *Mirror*, he'd received news that he had a
conditional place at Oxford. He was, said Straw, 'thoroughly
ashamed' at the embarrassment he had caused his father, and
had already gone with him to the police to make a voluntary

statement. He had been released on police bail, and it was not
yet clear if there would be charges. His son expected 'no
favours' from the legal system, Straw said. On the other hand,
he should not be made to suffer because his father was Home
Secretary.

Jack Straw went on to speak of his frustration at being
ordered to stay silent, and his relief at being able to comment
now. The call from the *Mirror*, he told the press, had been one
of his 'darkest hours' as a parent:

> Let me speak briefly as a father. When the *Mirror* first
> spoke to me I felt the same emotions as any parents
> would in such circumstances – shock and concern.
> Being a parent means giving love and support and –
> when it's necessary - confronting children with their
> wrongdoing. When a child does wrong, I believe it to be
> the duty of a parent to act promptly. That is what I
> sought to do . . . Of course I was embarrassed by this. I
> think any parent would be embarrassed by the informa-
> tion which I was given. But it doesn't change my
> attitude. It has been a period of considerable difficulty,
> just as it would have been for any other family. I have
> teenage children and I am aware of the pressures they
> are under and the parents of teenage children are under.
> I have always sought – and so have my colleagues – to
> conduct our family lives the same way as other people.
> These are experiences that other families have had and
> so it does not in any way affect my ability to talk on
> these matters.

If anything, the experience had 'hardened' his 'convictions'
about drugs, crime and the importance of responsible parenting.[18]

The scandal was an object lesson, too, for the press and the

public. Until that moment, New Labour thinking on parents
had not quite made sense. Or rather, no one had given much
thought to what 'responsible parenting' meant; it was just
another one of those catchphrases that floated around in the
media ether, to be invoked as a symbolic ideal when discussing parents who seemed to take no responsibility for their
children whatsoever. But here was someone who was not just
talking about responsible parenting; he was practising responsible parenting *and* talking about how hard it was to do. Not
only had the *Mirror* sting caused him pain and embarrassment, it had also required him to make some very difficult
judgement calls. There were conflicting duties. He had to
think about his responsibilities not only as a cabinet minister
but also as a citizen and father. As a father, he was responsible for teaching his son the difference between right and
wrong, but what degree of responsibility should a father of a
17-year-old take for his son? Take too much, and he won't
learn from his mistakes. Take too little, and he could be
crushed by them. There was also the tricky question as to
how you went about showing love and giving support to a
child who has caused you so much public embarrassment.
But Jack Straw was equal to this one, too. Instead of kicking
William out and telling him he was on his own this time, he'd
gone down to the police station with him, and then after that
he'd taken him home.

  To nurture, to educate, and to protect. According to the
American philosopher Sarah Ruddick, the practice of parenting boils down to these three things. They are always in
conflict. How you resolve these conflicts depends on the context. If your two-year-old is teetering on the window sill, you
will probably decide that this is not the time to let her learn
the hard way about the danger of heights. But if you have an
11-year-old who wants to go to school by herself, you will
probably decide that it would be wrong to overprotect her,

and better to teach her how to use the bus system. You are always making judgement calls. Because you're aware that your judgement calls could be wrong, you think about them, both before you make them and afterwards. You talk about them with other parents, and find out what they think and how they've handled similar problems. You develop better judgement through trial, error and open discussion. I learn from your mistakes, you learn from mine. Even if we're all in agreement that all responsible parents nurture, educate and protect, the question as to *how* you do these things is endlessly complicated, and to me, endlessly fascinating. Because it depends so much on context and because no two contexts are alike, there is no such thing as a perfect system. Even the most responsible parent is always learning. This means that no parent can afford to stand on a pedestal and say, I have it sussed. And it is a very foolhardy parent who points at a child and says, 'See? All my work has paid off!' Especially when they're teenagers, and even when they're adults, children have this way of showing you up.

All parents know all this from experience. They might not be in the habit of explicating it, but they can recognise 'responsible parenting' when they see it – and that, I think, is why the public response to Jack Straw's statement was so favourable. The consensus was that there should be no question of resignation. Straw had done the best he could under the circumstances. No parent had full control over a 17-year-old boy, anyway. It would be unfair, as the leader in the *Times* said, 'for the sins of the son to be visited on the father. If anything, Mr Straw may be able to do his job better now. His understanding of the problem of drugs, teenagers, parenting and youth justice will have been enhanced by his recent experience. And he has conducted himself with dignity and openness under pressure. Few who watched his performances on television yesterday could have failed to feel sympathy for his plight.' There was sympathy too for poor William, who would not have been set up, everyone agreed, had it not been for the fact that his father was Home Secretary. 'Now William should be left alone. He has already paid a heavy price.'[19]

An extraordinary number of MPs from other parties made statements to the same effect. Sir Brian Mawhinney, the Shadow Home Secretary, was one of them. Lord Steel, the former Liberal leader, was another. Nigel Evans, vice-chairman of the Parliamentary Drugs Misuse Group, said, 'If anything, this sad episode demonstrates that drugs can affect all families, irrespective of rank or class.'[20]

With time, it turned out to be not such a sad episode after all. It was, in fact, something of a watershed. Here, for perhaps the first time, we had a cabinet-rank politician, a *man*, talking about good parenting not as a lofty ideal, or a female calling, but as something he himself was engaged with. He spoke not as a lofty moral guide but as a 'practitioner'. He acknowledged how difficult it all was, while at the same time making it clear that there was nothing in life he considered more important.

The most amazing thing was that he was doing all this in public. Important women often talk of their fear at being 'taken less seriously as professionals' if they speak openly about their domestic concerns. It does not seem to be a fear that has ever plagued Jack Straw. He starts from the premise that anything he does *is* important, so why apologise? When Labour came into power, family policy was still the least important area of politics. It's largely because of Jack Straw that it began to travel from margin to centre.

In the autumn of 1997 – not long before the scandal, in fact – Tony Blair put Straw in charge of the Ministerial Group on the Family. After deliberating for a year, it published a consultation document, the first ever of its kind in this country, called *Supporting Families*. Much of what it outlined in this green paper was already law; in other areas it was seeking consultation. It provoked quite heated debate inside the policy world. But most people outside it – and that included the majority in the media – did not quite grasp how ambitious a project it was, nor how radically it could change the contract between parents and government, and so reshape the lives of all people with children.

The key message of *Supporting Families* is in its title. The government was undertaking to support parents in their work. If parents in Britain were severely stressed, it was because previous governments had left them to adjust to massive change in society and the economy on a case-by-case, ad hoc basis. Despite these governments' many fine speeches about the importance of family values, their own laissez-faire policies helped to make family breakdown more likely. A government that wanted families to be stronger and more stable had to *help* rather than hinder them. This help had to come in an entirely new form: 'Neither a "back to basics" fundamentalism, trying to turn back the clock, nor an "anything goes" liberalism which denies the fact that how families behave affects us all, is credible any more.'[21]

Family policy had to be complex – there was no longer any basis to this idea that you could 'affect how families behave' by pulling large policy levers. And it needed to depend less on rhetoric, and more on practical help.[22]

It was in this spirit that it proposed a family rescue package that concentrated on five different problem areas: the practice of parenting, child poverty, working parents, family breakdown, and severe family dysfunction. Its overall aims were to (1) give all families access to advice and education as and when they needed them; (2) give poorer families extra financial support, especially when they were bringing up very small children; (3) make the workplace adjust to the needs of working parents; (4) encourage marriage and help prevent family breakdown;

and (5) intervene early in families with serious problems like domestic violence, truancy and school-age pregnancy.

This help needed to be addressed to families as *they were today*. 'Family structure has become more complicated, with many more children living with step-parents or in single-parent households. Women increasingly want to work and have careers as well as being mothers. Many fathers want more involvement with their children's upbringing.'[23] But government involvement could not be value-free.

> A modern family policy . . . needs to be founded on clear principles. First, the interests of children must be paramount. This government's interest in family policy is primarily an interest in ensuring that the next generation gets the best possible start in life. Second, children need stability and security. Many lone parents and unmarried couples raise their children every bit as successfully as married parents. But marriage is still the surest foundation for raising children and remains the choice of the majority of people in Britain. We want to strengthen the institution of marriage to help more marriages succeed. Third, wherever possible, the government should offer support to all parents, so that they can better support children, rather than trying to substitute for parents. There needs to be a clear understanding of the rights and responsibilities which fall to families and to government. Parents raise children, and that is how things should remain. More direct intervention should only occur in extreme circumstances, for example in cases of domestic violence, or where the welfare of children is at stake.[24]

Even this had to be approached with trepidation, it prudently suggested. 'We in government need to approach family policy with a strong dose of humility. We must not preach and we must not give the impression that members of the government are any better than the rest of the population in meeting the challenge of family life. They are not.'[25]

This was one of the boldest statements in the document. In seeking to put members of the government on a level playing field with 'the rest of the population', it was breaking with an ancient tradition of family policy, the upstairs-downstairs tradition in which respectable gentlemen who never got their hands dirty handed down directions for the wives, servants and slaves of the world to live by.

Just as important was its break with the dark and creepy media obsession with wicked families and criminal parents. Here, finally, was something specifically designed for parents who were trying hard already and who could only do better with a bit of help. Instead of urging those parents to 'hold back the waves', and return to old family forms and traditional values, it sought to find ways of modernising those values so that parents in new family forms could also live by them. Thus, it was addressed to women who were not just mothers, and fathers who were not just breadwinners, and it acknowledged that while both groups had special problems, neither set of problems would be solved unless they were both solved together. There was an acknowledgement, too, that the problems were not just economic and not just structural. Even if everyone agreed that there was more than one possible form a family could take, the fact remained that all families with children had a common purpose – to give them the best possible start in life. So it was just as important to develop a better understanding of how the practice of parenting actually worked. To this end, the green paper proposed a National Family and Parenting Institute. Although it would be government funded, we were assured it would be designed to 'bite the hand that feeds it'.[26]

Very, *very* enlightened, in other words – which may explain
why the media swallowed the new medicine so meekly. There
was concern expressed in some quarters (most emphatically
in the *Guardian* and the *Observer*) about the document's affir-
mation of marriage: this could only mean that married
parents would be better served by government policies than
would unmarried parents. Lone-parent pressure groups complained about the implied vote of no confidence for those
bringing up their children alone. Gay and lesbian groups criticised Straw's opposition to homosexuals adopting children or
lesbians having children via IVF and AID (artificial insemination by donor).[27] Peter Lilley, deputy leader of the Tories,
took issue with the stress on family intervention. In his view,
this skirted the issue: 'Once we strip away the social workers'
list-wish of new ways to badger families, there are actually
very few measures in this document that will help to
strengthen the institutions of marriage and family life.'[28]

But church leaders were more receptive. Cardinal Basil
Hume went so far as to say that he hoped the document
would 'prompt a soul-searching debate through society' on
parental commitment and the importance of marriage. 'The
mounting social and economic costs of family breakdown,
not least the often deep and lasting effects on children, must
be a matter of grave public concern, and therefore of public
policy, as well as of private distress.'[29]

A leader in the *Sunday Times* congratulated Straw and his
fellow ministers for 'courage, in face of progressive
protests . . . to admit that marriage is the best way for two
adults to raise their children – and to assert that the State
should intervene in family life only "in extreme circumstances". But care as well as bravery will be needed to
develop policies that achieve these aims without meddling in
people's everyday lives or turning ministers into vicars.' It
noted that while some of the proposals gave couples and

families 'a chance to make their own choices about their lives', others risked 'giving the State new opportunities to interfere in marriages and in the way in which parents bring up their children'. And while there might be a 'clear need' for a new National Family and Parenting Institute, 'careful scrutiny will be required to prevent it from turning into a nanny state'.

It concluded that most of the green paper constituted 'a worthwhile effort to shore up family life. Yet family stability is best bolstered when parents have jobs and children receive a good education, fostering independence from the State. The family is a bastion against an intrusive State and a shelter from the demands of modern life.' Thus, in the long run, 'money spent on moving parents from welfare to work and improving school standards for children' was likely to produce more good outcomes than money spent on improving parents and parenting skills.[30]

At a consultation exercise organised by the Family Policy Studies Centre in February 1999, there were graver doubts expressed – this despite the fact that it was attended largely by people working in professions, charities and agencies that stood to gain from the proposed policies. Many felt that the government was making broad assumptions about parents, children, marriage and divorce that were not well supported by available data; this meant that some of the policies that the green paper was proposing were based more on wishful thinking than on good evidence.

While there was a consensus that the document was ambitious, written in the right spirit and an important first step, people were worried that the project might fail and then be discredited because it overstated its case. For example, no one yet knew for sure how effective counselling and parenting education really was. It was even hard to know which types worked and which did not.

There was concern, too, about the green paper's insistence that it was 'inclusive'. This seemed to be more an expression of good intentions than a statement of fact. In aiming to think inclusively, the authors of the paper had overlooked a number of conflicts of interest. For example, it was all very well to say that fathers needed to be involved with their children. But the green paper also supported efforts to end domestic violence, and therefore supported any measures that kept fathers with a history of violence away from children. How did these two policies fit together?

Money was another sticking point. Although everyone conceded that the government was pouring a lot of money into the national childcare strategy and parenting education, and putting a lot of thought into ways of supporting poorer families, many felt it was nowhere near enough to make a real difference to parents' and children's lives. There were not enough teeth in the measures to promote fairness at work, either. The prediction was that most employers would be able to continue to be just as family-unfriendly as they are now.

There was more than a little concern about the green paper's use of the word 'support'. The definition was very broad – it meant everything from low-key, informal, optional advice to some pretty harsh interventions that involved the police and punished non-compliance with heavy fines. Some of these harsher measures were so clumsily designed that they could easily exacerbate the very problems they were meant to solve. If, for example, you tried to get a stepfather to 'knock' a recalcitrant 16-year-old boy into shape by issuing a parenting order, you increased the chances of his trying to solve the problem with violence. If you then slapped him with a £1,000 fine, the stepfather's response was likely to be to 'show the boy the door'.

Some objected to the vilification of violent boys and teenage girls and were keen that these folk myths did not carry over into policy. The abolition of *doli incapax* (the law which held that children aged 10–13 were 'incapable of evil') was, some feared, bound to make it easier, not harder, to scapegoat young people deemed antisocial. Others expressed worries about the way in which the government might be planning to deploy its army of parent advisers and educators. How to ensure that parent education remained a voluntary option? How to protect confidentiality for those who sought help from counsellors, health visitors and helplines? If the government planned to increase its intervention into family life, then it was very important to know exactly where and how the government drew and redrew the line between parents it identified as 'normal' and those it identified as needing intervention. It was not clear who decided such things. And so it was worrying that the standards this unknown quantity was setting for parents were so high. While he, she or it was careful never to draw a direct link between good parenting and a good society, the suggestion was that well-parented children were those who became good citizens. If parents failed to deliver those good citizens, who would be held to account?

This, in my view, is the most important question of them all. Let me try to explain why.

What is wrong with this picture?

Being a parent is a challenging job. Many parents get by through a combination of instinct, advice, reading and family support, but this is not always enough.[31]

Parents need a great deal of help around the birth of their children.[32]

Parents sometimes need help to enforce discipline.[33]

Some parents need support and direction in fulfilling their responsibilities and in helping to prevent a child or young person from turning to crime.[34]

Children who grow up in stable, successful families are less likely to become involved in offending.[35]

All of these statements come from *Supporting Families*. I've chosen them for my thought experiment because they are statements with which I more or less agree.

The first three I know to be true from my own experience. I knew nothing about children when I had my first child. I did manage to muddle through. But I wouldn't have done so if it had not been for a health visitor who did far more for me than her job description required. In the years that followed, there were many other transitions I had a hard time coping with. I had to move often when my first two children were little, and this led to much social isolation.

I went into a depression when my marriage was breaking up. After the divorce, there were four years when I was earning less than £5,000 a year. In the fifth year, I did better, but then I set up house with the father of my two younger children, and in the space of twenty months I went from being a single mother of two to being the main breadwinner for a family of eight.

I have never had a steady income, even though I have almost always worked. I have never been entitled to maternity leave and could not afford a pension until just a few months ago. But I have been very fortunate in my friends, who made the difference during my twenty years of rough patches. I've had plenty of therapy and counselling, too; although a lot of it was useless, there were two people I saw who made a real difference. I don't know where I would be now without them.

I've always put my children at the centre of my life. I've arranged my work life around them. And so, to a much larger degree than is said to be normal, have their fathers. None of us have families in this country, but that never meant that we were bringing up the children alone; there have always been plenty of babysitters, childminders and teachers. People seldom take a unified view of all the people a child will know and depend on in the course of a normal childhood. They tend to fixate instead on the central relationships with the mother or father. But common sense tells you that it takes a huge array of people to bring a child to adulthood. I might have final responsibility as my children's mother, but I have never had sole responsibility, and neither has any other parent I know.

Another thing I know from experience: a timely piece of good advice can stop a minor problem you're having with a child from turning into an insurmountable problem. I have no trouble with the idea that parents should have access to education and support. And so I like the proposal that parent education should not be a one-off deal for people struggling with their first baby, I know only too well that each new stage of family life brings a new set of problems, and no matter how much experience you have, there will always be something that knocks you off your feet. So I have no particular trouble with the following quotes, all of which are also in the green paper:

The early years of a child's life are critical to their future success and happiness. We are determined to invest in better opportunities for our youngest children and to support parents in preparing them to succeed at school and in life.[36]

Many parents are uncertain about what to expect at each stage of their child's development and would welcome the additional support and expert advice on a range of parenting issues which health visitors are able to give.[37]

Parent Network runs courses for parents covering relationship skills – listening, negotiating, setting boundaries and assertiveness.[38]

One of the most difficult skills for parents is to apply a consistent and appropriate level of discipline to their children.[39]

Helping parents to exercise effective care and supervision of their children can achieve long-term benefits by reducing the risk that children will become involved in delinquent or offending behaviour.[40]

The tone might be a little stern, but there are many occasions over the past twenty years when I would have welcomed the steady, consistent, responsive and evidence-based support services they imply. And it's not just the support itself, it's the acknowledgement of the kinds of supports parents need today. Let me give an example of what it's like to be living in a society which refuses that acknowledgement. Once, during my single mother phase, I went into casualty to have the doctors look at an inflamed cyst on my back and, to my surprise, they said they had to operate at once. As they began to prepare me for surgery, I asked them if they could help me make arrangements for my children to be collected from school and cared for over the night. The answer was no; they told me the only person they could contact for me was my next of kin. But then it emerged that, according to their definition of kin, there was no one in the country I could call. However, they still refused to get in touch with anyone else; they said their job was to save my life, not to make childcare arrangements. Following this line of reasoning, I was eventually able to get them to ring my GP. Happily for me, she was a very close friend, so she was the one who collected the children and took care of them until I got out of hospital.

But I should not have had to scramble like that. I shouldn't have had to be lying in a cubicle in a paper gown, wondering what would happen to my children if no one turned up to collect them after school. The doctors did not mean any harm, they were only doing their job. But to them, patients were autonomous individuals. They had not been trained to factor in that patient's caring responsibilities when scheduling an operation. They assumed a staff of invisible others who were always on hand to jump in and pick up these responsibilities as and when needed. It's not just doctors who suffer from this kind of social blindness. Our entire work culture, our school system, our political and public institutions and the philosophical ideas that shaped them, all assume the same unlimited pool of invisible carers. By assuming it, they of course depend on it; but by refusing to acknowledge it, they can deny that they do. This is extremely frustrating if you happen to *be* a carer. So it's very, very gratifying to read a government document that makes caring work visible, and that acknowledges its social importance.

It doesn't just call it important. It calls it a *job*, a job that mothers cannot and do not do alone. It's gratifying to read a government document and see fathers acknowledged as well as mothers – to see the words 'parents need' instead of 'mothers should'. The word 'parent' has a nice, neutral ring to it. It seems fair, too, as it gives equal consideration to mothers and fathers. It implies that all is not sex war; that while mothers and fathers have separate interests, and special problems, there are also numerous problems, interests, needs and aims that they share. It's an acknowledgement that we've moved on, that society has changed in ways that are beyond our control, and that we need to find not just new ways of bringing up children but also of instilling our cultural values into the next generation.

The word parent also allows us to escape the old circular debate about what mothers should do, and father's don't do, or mothers want to do, or fathers say they would like to do but don't. It paves the way for a larger debate about what mothers and fathers can expect from society, and what society expects from them. Once you look at things from this perspective, it is obvious that it's not just mothers and fathers who have a common interest. Parents and governments have a common aim: to give the next generation the best possible start in life.

But here we begin to see a problem. The word parent implies the existence of children without actually bringing them into focus. Let's look again at some of those statements from the green paper, to see how children appear in them:

Parents need a great deal of help around the birth of their *children*.

Many parents are uncertain about what to expect at each stage of their *child's* development and would welcome the additional support and expert advice on a range of parenting issues which health visitors are able to give.

One of the most difficult skills for parents is to apply a consistent and appropriate level of discipline to their *children*.

Some parents need support and direction in fulfilling their responsibilities and in helping prevent a *child* or *young person* from turning to crime.

Children who grow up in stable, successful families are less likely to become involved in offending.

The children implied in these statements live in a very different world from those implied by the UN Convention on the Rights of the Child. Their voices and viewpoints count for very little; it is for adults to decide what is in their best interest without wasting too much time on consultation. Questions around their happiness and well-being are important but not paramount. Children are measured and judged primarily by their behaviour and performance. When the word 'happiness' appears, it is paired with the word 'success'. When the word 'loving' appears, it is to modify the word 'firmness'. Bringing up children is not a joy or a revelation, but a service. Children are not little people with their own personalities that transform the way you look at the world. They feature instead as challenging and problematic objects that must be monitored, corralled, tamed and endlessly improved.

While this may be an accurate description of some aspects of child-rearing, as a *general* description it is narrow and blinkered and does not come close to describing what it means to me or, I suspect, what it means to anyone who has ever looked after children. Why is it so narrow? There is, of course, a perfectly good reason. The authors of the green paper are only interested in those aspects of child-rearing that make it a job of social importance. This becomes very clear if you take some of those statements from the paper and replace the word 'parents' with a word that comes to us from the workplace:

Being a *line manager* is a challenging job. Many *line managers* get by through a combination of instinct, advice, reading and *peer* support, but this is not always enough.

One of the most difficult skills for *line managers* is to apply a consistent and appropriate level of discipline to their *subordinates*.

Line managers sometimes need help to enforce discipline.

Some *line managers* need support and direction in fulfilling their responsibilities and in helping prevent *their subordinates* from turning to crime.

The Network for Better Business runs courses for *line managers* covering relationship skills – listening, negotiating, setting boundaries and assertiveness.

That these substitutions work so well is an indication of how keen the green paper is to define parents in the language of the workplace. A parent's job, then, is not to bring up children according to their own ideas of right and wrong, but according to standards that are set by the state. The line-manager parent does have a certain degree of power, but he is also accountable to higher authorities. He must deliver the goods, and if they're not up to standard he risks losing his job.

This is the understanding at the core of the new parent-state contract: you do your job right, or you're out. The implied threat is one that any parent would find alarming. But it is not something I would really want to argue with. I would not, for example, want my children to be at my mercy if I suddenly lost my mind and went off to Spain for a holiday, or subjected them to a violent boyfriend, or bundled them up and abandoned them in a nearby copse. It is something of a comfort to know that other people will step in and take over the care of your children if you are no longer competent.

But no one is ever *just* a parent. It is not a term that implies a whole person, or defines an entire life. People who are parents are employees when they go to work, consumers when they go shopping, members of the viewing public when they turn on the television, and citizens when they vote. The word parent implies not just a person but an activity. Because no one is a parent without a child, the word parent also implies a relationship and a set of obligations. This brings us to another problem with the new social contract proposed in the green paper, which begins to become clear when you take the statements from the green paper, and replace the word 'parent' with more traditional terms:

> Being a *mother and homemaker* is a job many women find challenging. Many women get by through a combination of instinct, advice, reading and family support, but this is not always enough.

> *Mothers* need a great deal of help around the birth of their children.

> *Women* sometimes need men to help them enforce discipline.

> Some *mothers* need *male* support and direction in fulfilling their responsibilities and in helping prevent a child or young person from turning to crime.

> Children who grow up in stable, successful families with

stay-at-home *mothers* are less likely to become involved in offending.

Pick up any childcare book dated before 1970, and you'll find statements like these on almost every page. Pick up most childcare books from the past twenty-five years, and you'll see that the majority of experts have moved on to more gender-sensitive language. My first thought when I look at the substitutions I've just done is, heavens, how did the old guys ever get away with this degree of condescension? Why did no one notice the benevolent paternalism oozing out of every word? The world suggested by them is one in which women are too silly to think for themselves, and doctors and fathers know best, and children go astray unless their mothers devote themselves to their best interests 24 hours a day. It's a world where women's rights matter little, and their needs as individuals fade in the background. All that matters is the quality of their service as wives, homemakers and mothers.

This is a world that doesn't exist any more, but now suddenly, here they are again – the same sentiments, but phrased in such a way that you don't immediately notice. It might seem to be fairer and more dignified to require that all parents devote themselves selflessly to the care and support of their children, instead of saying that all mothers must put their children first and all fathers must be breadwinners. But then you remember that even though so many women work now, still it is mostly women who care for children. Even if a policy is designed for 'parents' instead of 'mothers', most of the people it affects *are* mothers. So to use the word parent is to pretend that we've moved on, while maintaining the same condescending view of mothers and mothering.

That said, any policy designed for parents and not just mothers does redefine fathers and fathering. But from a man's point of view, it's hardly a promotion. Mothers and fathers have gone through huge changes over the past generation, but the status our society accords to people who care for children is much the same, which means active fathers have as little status as active mothers.

And so it is that this radical proposal for a new partnership between parents and the state is in some ways terribly old-fashioned. It still assumes that mothers cannot be trusted to make their own decisions, and that they need not be consulted on matters of policy that might affect them. It rewards men who want to be active fathers by marginalising them just as much as it marginalises mothers.

This might seem like a strange thing to say about a document called *Supporting Families*. Unless, perhaps, you extend the thought experiment to the title and imagine the conclusions you might draw if it were called 'Supporting Mothers' or 'Supporting Dependent Wives'. The true meaning of the word 'support' becomes clear if you look between the lines of the document and make a list of all the things it *doesn't* suggest.

One thing it does not suggest is that parents might be a source of information, insight or good ideas. The assumption is that the state can define that all by itself, with possible recourse to experts and expert organisations if necessary. Nowhere is there a suggestion that ideas about the practice of parenting should arise out of discussions with people who actually do practise it. The ideas begin at the top, and then they stay there.

Another thing it does not suggest is that the world of parenting is a world not just of common aims, but also of conflicting interests. It provides no mechanism for parents to negotiate those conflicting interests. In other words, it assumes that parents are a lot like children. The difference is that they never quite grow up. Which is why they must be

supported . . . and why, at the end of the day, they have no
political power.

What's missing from this picture?

Years ago, a lawyer I knew went to observe a trial in a Middle
Eastern country on behalf of a human rights organisation. It
was a confusing experience, because he knew nothing about
the law in that country, could not speak the language, and
could not find a single person who was willing to be his inter-
preter. But in the end he decided that as he was there anyway,
he might as well attend the trial. From the moment he set foot
in the courtroom, he was immediately aware that there was
something deeply wrong about the scene he was witnessing.
He spent the entire morning trying to work out what it was.
It wasn't until just before they adjourned for lunch that it
suddenly occurred to him that the courtroom was missing a
witness stand.

That's how I feel about the new family policies – that they
come to us out of a room that is lacking a witness stand.
Many of the people in that room have been at pains to consult
with parents at every juncture, to take their views into
account, and to represent the interests of parents who do not
have the wherewithal to represent themselves. But the consulting, the listening and the representing have taken place
inside a framework that ordinary parents played no part in
designing. The room where the decisions are made is for
professionals only.

The policies that have been coming out of this room
cannot form the basis of an equal partnership between families and the state – for the simple reason that it is designed
primarily to suit the interests of the state. Despite the language of inclusion they offer two sets of policies: one for

'successful' families and the other for 'families with serious problems'. These definitions are not set by the families themselves but, once again, by the state. There is no mechanism for parents who might want to challenge those definitions, or even just know who exactly is setting them.

Likewise, there is no procedure for parents who feel unjustly treated, nor for parents who want to question the policies that shape their lives, or offer up constructive criticism. These are policies that allow too many important decisions to be made in that room at the top, by faceless people, behind closed doors.

If the policies were more democratic in structure, if they allowed for a two-way conversation between families and the state, then there would be nothing to fear about the mass enlistment of counsellors and parent educators to the already impressive array of guardians charged with overseeing family life. But because they will be operating within a framework that gives the state final authority, it is a little worrying that *Supporting Families* is proposing a cradle-to-grave service.

It is even more worrying when you think about the government's obsession with 'bad parents'. It may not be the originator of the panics we have considered in this book, but all too often its representatives have been very happy to go with the flow. When vigilante gangs go after paedophiles they say yes, we understand, and that is why there must be tighter controls. They condone the panics about violent teenage boys and call for them to be more tightly controlled; they also intervene in the anxieties about underage pregnant girls, especially the part about the need for more stringent controls. They routinely berate parents in the plural about their lazy, selfish ways: this sort of parent should also, in their view, be subject to tighter controls, and they routinely encourage children to name and shame neglectful and abusive parents, so that they can be promptly brought to justice and corrected.

These tirades put all the fine talk about the 'good-enough parent' into perspective. In the present climate, who could dare to claim they were one of these? Never have the odds against good-enough parenting been greater. The standards of performance are rising, just as more mothers are being pushed into work. The definitions of neglect and abuse are growing, and now extend to include cohabitation and marriage breakdown. In the present climate, to speak in public as a good-enough parent is to invite someone else to point out how abysmally we've failed. And so we leave this risky business to the few brave lobby groups that dare, and keep our peace. This makes us an insecure and biddable constituency, quick to apologise for our faults and slow to point out where our masters could do better, and the government has taken advantage of our weaknesses to consolidate its power.

Once upon a time, there was at least one type of parent who could expect to be heard when he represented his family's interests in the public arena. He was known as the head of the household and/or the breadwinner, and he could speak out on behalf of his family without endangering his position as very important citizen, autonomous political actor, and man of the world. He was more likely than not to be middle-class, and almost always white. He had a very high opinion of himself – much too high, we would say now. But he did have his uses. One of the most useful things about him was that he saw his role as head of household not just in terms of responsibilities but also in terms of entitlements. He had no qualms about standing up when the government failed to give adequate institutional support to family life and saying, 'This is disgraceful. I have a family to feed, a mortgage to pay, a son to educate, a daughter to prepare for marriage.'

It would be a very foolish man who would stand up and give that speech today. The head of household-cum-breadwinner has lost his moral credibility. His brand of benevolent paternalism now stands for the oppression of wives and daughters, authoritarian discipline, and a license for abuse. But with the departure of the male head of household from the family constellation, something very strange happened. Families have lost their one route into public debate. They turned into *headless* households. We've arrived at a point where *no* parent can speak as an upstanding citizen. In the political arena we're not just headless, but also voiceless.

A parent's point of view

But since this is my book, I can perhaps pretend for a few moments that this is not so. I can imagine that I am inside the room where all the important decisions are made, that this room has now been furnished with a witness stand and that I am standing in it, and that my brief today is not to pull a consultation document to shreds but to suggest that its authors set it inside a bigger and bolder framework.

So my first job is to explain why I think the framework within which they are working now tells only half the story. Although it is a good reflection of the problems of the modern family as perceived by civil servants, politicians and some professionals, it does not try to see these overall problems from a parent's point of view. Although it draws upon good research about family life – and also, presumably, information gleaned from focus groups – the scope of these enquiries is, from a parent's point of view, far too narrow.

If you sent every parent in the country a blank piece of paper and asked them to write down what *they* thought their biggest problems were, you would find that they too would touch upon all the areas covered by the new family policies. They would agree that there was a need for more education and support, both emotional and material. They would agree that they needed help with childcare, and with balancing home and work commitments. They would be forced to admit that families were hard to keep together, especially when they were grappling with serious problems like juvenile delinquency, abuse and teenage pregnancy, and that life after divorce was, if anything, even harder to manage than a failing marriage.

But they would also touch on other problems that neither begin nor end at home. They would say what a shame it is that children can't play outside by themselves any more, because of the danger posed by heavy traffic and speeding cars. They would talk about the insane compromises they have had to make in order to care and provide for their children properly. They would speak about insensitive, inflexible institutions – schools that are blind to the needs of working parents, employers who assume all working parents have an invisible 'other' taking care of the home front, tax systems that disadvantage families where there is a stay-at-home parent, health services that respond too slowly or not at all when they are concerned about their children's emotional well-being and are seeking professional help. They would ask difficult questions. For example, how can this government go on and on about how important it is for parents to devote more time and energy to their children, when at the same time it is trying to push all parents back into work? And how can it say that it believes all children deserve to be in regular touch with both parents, while its own court system seems happy to exclude some parents at the drop of a hat?

These questions point to problems in the structure of national institutions – schools, health services, banks, employers, courts. They reveal contradictions in government policies and also yawning gaps in strategy. If you sent a copy of *Supporting Families* to every parent in the country, and asked them how much they address these problems, you'd hear that, yes, they saw these measures as steps in the right direction, but only very little steps. They would say, for example, that a toothless public relations exercise was not enough to make the workplace family-friendly, and that the steps to help families with childcare costs were well-meaning but pitifully inadequate.

They would ask questions about the language. For example, the desire to 'respect diversity'. How exactly were these policies addressing this? They would say that the world they lived in was very diverse, and riddled with ideological strife, not just between people from different classes and ethic backgrounds but also between stay-at-home mothers and working mothers, married families and divorced parents, mothers and fathers. They would say that it was important that all these people find a way to live together, and establish a consensus about what counted for good parenting. But they would also say that we are far from that consensus at the moment, and so should not pretend that it already exists.

The main problem with this document, in other words, is that it fails to reflect the world of parenting as parents themselves experience it. There is no real sense of the problems they grapple with day in and day out, and no acknowledgement that, having grappled with them for so long, they might have some constructive ideas about how to solve them.

But if the great and the good really want to make parents part of the solution, it is not enough for them to sit here in this room, patiently listening to parents' voices. When they draft their policies, they also have to take the parent's point of view. In other words, they need to approach the problems of modern family life as if they had just brought a child into the world and were trying to figure out how to get this child from here to age eighteen.

Although no two parents are alike, there *is* a common question: how to care for my child, and care for my child

well? Just to ask this question is to see the problems of family
life in a new way. Things that seemed very important when
you were just looking in from the outside, begin to fade away.
Labels like single mother, working mother and stay-at-home
mother, traditional father, active father and stepfather, cease
to define discrete categories. It becomes clear that most parents float in and out of these categories and back again, and
that no matter what label they happen to be living under
at a particular time, there are some problems that remain
constant.

When you're standing on the outside looking in, it's 'problem carers' who cause the greatest worry. But if you take a
'parent's point of view', the main worry is what you might call
the 'problem of care'.

This is the American political philosopher Joan Tronto's
definition of care: 'to maintain, continue and repair the world
so that we can live in it as well as possible.'[41] It's a definition
that covers traditional unpaid women's work and also the
work done by, for example, nurses, domestic servants, childcare workers, office cleaners, cooks, rubbish collectors,
famine relief workers and environmentalists. Tronto defines
four stages of care – seeing the need for it, taking steps to
meet that need, the actual giving of care, and care receiving.
Caring well is a *practice*, not a principle or an emotion. To
care well, you have to be attentive, responsible, competent
and responsive. Good intentions are not enough. You need a
'deep and thoughtful knowledge of the situation and all of the
actors' situations, needs, and competencies . . . Carers must
make judgements about needs, conflicting needs, strategies
for achieving ends' and ways of listening and responding to
the people they are caring for.[42]

Caring well is a difficult practice fraught with moral dilemmas. You can provide such thorough care for someone else
that you leave your own basic needs unmet; you can subject

your charges to danger by neglecting them; you can give highly competent care that is very upsetting to the care-receiver, or that exploits her vulnerability. No care-giver can ever meet the ideal. But by measuring everyday care against an ethic that defines the importance of attentiveness, responsibility, competence and responsiveness, at least you have a way of understanding how well you are doing, of seeing how you might improve it. You also have a way of elaborating standards, and these form the basis of an 'ethic of care'.[43]

This, in turn, makes it possible to discuss care publicly and politically. Once we have a clear idea of the ethic of care, 'we can use this concept to review our own daily activities and notice that care consumes a large part of our daily lives'. And yet there is no systematic study of care. Our understanding of it is fragmented. According to Tronto, this is not the result of a deliberate conspiracy. Rather, it's because in 'our present culture there is a great ideological advantage to gain from keeping care from coming into focus. By not noticing how pervasive and central care is to human life, those who are in positions of power and privilege can continue to ignore and to degrade the activities of care in our society.'[44]

If, however, you take the carer's point of view, you have no choice but to question even your most basic political assumptions. One conclusion she has drawn herself is that our present assumption that 'all men are created equal' only works well for rich, healthy and autonomous adults, and works against the interests of all others. 'Throughout our lives all of us go through varying degrees of dependence and independence, and autonomy and vulnerability.' In her view, the young and the weak are not well served by the fiction that we are all men, and as men created equal.[45] What she suggests instead is that we think of equality as an ideal – something we work towards, instead of assuming it is already there.

Thus, the aim of good childcare is to bring a child to the point where he can become independent and autonomous. If equality is an ideal to work towards, then the aim of caring for the weak, the elderly and the ill is to get them as close to that same ideal as is physically possible, while also giving them special protection that reflects the nature and degree of their dependence and vulnerability. By discussing care as something that helps people to achieve full citizenship, it finally becomes possible to make it clear how everyone in our society depends on it. And once having established the centrality of caring work, you can begin to argue for a better deal for life's carers.

You can, that is, if you have a political voice. So the first step in that process has to be to ensure that the political discussion of care is an enlightened and democratic one. Thus, family policy will be enlightened and democratic only if it draws from the discussions that parents have amongst themselves about the work they do, and if it reflects the principles and solutions that emerge from those discussions. When policies and programmes for parents arise out of the practice of parenting, when parents are invited to participate in discussions about their children and their communities not just as 'problems' but as experts in their own right, amazing things can happen. Let me illustrate this point with three examples. Two are success stories. The third is about a missed opportunity.

Three examples

The first comes from what is known as the 'hard end' of the parent education business, the place where parents could be said to have no power at all. The story is about parenting orders, which became law with the Crime and Disorder Act

1998, and formed part of an ambitious package of new measures that were further elaborated in the Youth Justice and
Criminal Evidence Act 1999. Each individual order is tailored to the child, but all include a 12-week parenting skills
course. Parents who fail to turn up could end up back in
court, facing fines of up to £1,000.

In October 1998, the orders were piloted by youth offending teams in nine different authorities. But even before the
pilots began, there was already much concern being expressed
about them by magistrates and civil rights groups. They
wanted to know why we were suddenly in the business of
punishing parents who are already deprived, stigmatised and
vulnerable. There was doubt, too, as to whether or not
mandatory lessons would even work. A Family Policy Studies
Centre briefing paper pointed out that there was also a danger
that parenting orders could exacerbate tensions in families
that are already under stress.[46]

All these questions are important, but so too are the questions that emerge once you've heard what parenting lessons
are like on the receiving end.

In September 1999, I was able to meet three women, all
mothers of young offenders, who have taken part in the pilot
programme set up by the Sunderland Youth Offending Team.
None, by the way, looked anything like your stereotypical
mother-of-a-young-offender. They were bright, capable,
responsible, 'in charge'. Everything about their appearance
said, 'I am worthy of respect'. The first, whose name was Jan,
had three children aged 20, 18 and 13: it was the middle one
who was in trouble. He had been one of fifty-odd cases 'on the
books' when the pilot started: Jan was one of eleven mothers
who had agreed to 'jump the gun' and attend the first course
on a voluntary basis.

The second was Sharon, mother of four and now expecting
her fifth: again only one of her children, the 15-year-old, was

in trouble, but he had been in so much trouble that she was in court with him every week.

The third woman, Mary, had only just been served with a parenting order. Her 15-year-old son Richard had only recently started to offend. She had not attended any classes yet: instead she had chosen to work with Lisa Robson, the Youth Offending Team's development officer, on a one-to-one basis. Her ex-husband was also seeing Robson, but separately.

When I asked her what she thought of it all, she caught her breath, then laughed and said it was all too much to take in, and too early to say. According to Lisa Robson, the first news of a parenting order was often a terrible shock to parents. But Jan and Sharon both told me they had been at their wits' end by this time, and so ready to consider anything. 'I've got a problem with Lee because he's handicapped as well,' said Jan. 'So he thinks if I'm going to be one of the lads I've got to do what they're doing.' Sharon nodded. 'I was going to court every week,' she said. 'Every night I was waiting for the knock on the door.'

And so off they went to their classes where, to their surprise, they found themselves amongst friends. 'When you first entered that room,' said Jan, 'straight away there was trust amongst us.'

'The one thing the Youth Justice never did,' said Jan, 'they never judged you by what went on. They judged you for the person you are. For me that was the best bit. I never got judged for my background, or the kids' background. I would say for the first time in my life I've been treated fairly.'

'The Youth Justice educated *me* more, and it made me turn around and educate the kids. And since then everything's worked for me. And with Lee, slowly but surely, I feel as if we're getting somewhere.' 'It helps,' said Sharon, 'because it's somebody who knows what you're going through. You're not on your own, and some of them have more experience than you have and you can learn from them.'

By the time Jan's course ended, it was clear to her and the other mothers that one of the reasons why so many of their children were getting into drugs, robbing houses and stealing cars was that they had 'nothing to do'. So with the help of the Youth Offending Team they'd got together the funding to take the old Salvation Army building on their estate and turn it into a youth centre. The most popular activity they ran was the weekly disco. They'd kept things simple: 'a bit of tuck shop, a bit of music . . . but the kids loved it. To be getting nineteen-year-old boys off the streets, it has to be pretty good.' They did still get a 'bit of bother coming through the door' but this was easily handled, because the mothers involved had known all the teenagers since they were babies and so were wise to all their tricks. Once they'd started the disco, 'the crime rate dropped every Monday night! Literally dropped! Drastically!'

When I asked her why she thought no one had tried out this idea before, she said, 'Well, there wasn't any Youth Justice before!' She still met mothers who were apprehensive about the orders, but the word of mouth about the classes had been so positive that women whose children are not offenders have asked her if they can come along too. And it's a shame when you've got to say, 'Oh, sorry, but you can't because your kid hasn't been in bother!'

How to explain these results? The credit must go to the people who've designed and led the courses. Helen Watson, the YOT Manager, told me that the last thing they'd wanted to do was alienate parents who were already struggling so hard, and with so many things working against them. So they had gone for a 'two-tier' programme that offered as much as possible on a voluntary basis and used parenting orders only when it was clear that there was no other way to bring parents in. Once the parents had come in, they'd gone out of their way to make it clear that they were not there to

punish them but to help them. The idea was not only to
help them cope with their difficult children, but also
to encourage them to set up networks and mentoring
schemes so that they could assist each other after the classes
came to an end. 'We see ongoing support as essential,' Helen
Watson told me.

Lisa Robson was keen to point out that this support had
turned out to be a two-way thing. Now that the team was in
regular contact with so many women in the community, they
had a much clearer idea about what life was like in those
communities, and what the real problems were.

One problem that was far more serious than they'd imagined was domestic violence. There have been numerous
instances in which women have gone home bursting with
new ideas, only to find that the man of the house is having
none of it. Where there is already a history of domestic violence, said Lisa Robson, parenting classes can make the
problem even worse.

At the time I met them, the Sunderland team was running
separate groups for fathers, but along the same principles.
Their remit as they saw it was not to address them as husbands, but to offer support and encouragement in their
capacity as fathers. The problem of domestic violence, they
had decided, needed to be addressed in another place, at
another time. But they had fewer fathers to work with
because fathers were less likely to be served with parenting
orders. You had to be in court with your child to be served
with the order, and the job of taking a child to court almost
always fell to the mother.

The team had been able to persuade magistrates to send
out summonses to fathers so that they were obliged to come
to court as well. But there was another complication: the
majority of young offenders on their books live in step-
families.

All three of the women I met were living with new partners. Sharon's new partner had been keen to treat her children
as his own and had said he would like to go to parenting
classes with her. The boy had also built up a very close relationship with the team and it was, she thought, because he
had all these things working in his favour that he was showing real signs of improvement. 'He's really calmed down. It's
like people are willing to help him. It's given him more self
confidence.'

But Jan said her husband didn't see her children as his problem, and he had already made it clear that he was not about to
attend any lessons. She thought this a great shame, as did the
others. 'It's nice,' Sharon said, 'when you have a man who can
come along and help because it does make it somehow that a
man's behind you. Sometimes you do need a man in a situation. If there's a father there, he *should* be involved.'

But as a rule, they said, the fathers were digging their heels
in and saying their children's and stepchildren's behaviour
had nothing to do with them. 'There are lots of women
coming forward and saying, I'll do this, I'll do that,' Jan said,
'but very few men.' She was hoping that this would change if
the team could bring more men into their programme. 'I
think if they heard from a friend who said, it's not bad, that
then . . .'

I asked how was anyone going to involve men in the first
instance, if they didn't want to become involved? The women
met my question with peals of laughter, and then Jan said,
'That's where the compulsory bit comes into it!' But it's not at
all clear that the methods which have worked so well for the
mothers will work in just the same way for the fathers. What's
clear is that in offering a programme that treated parents as
resources, the Sunderland team has discovered things which
have challenged and radically altered the way they see the
community they serve.

I saw the same thing happening in another new programme on the 'hard end' of the business, restorative justice.
In December 1999, I attended a meeting at a police head-
quarters in the Midlands at which six teenage boys who had
been implicated in a burglary had a meeting with members of
the family they had robbed. Also present were eight of their
parents – as many fathers as mothers in this instance – as well
as two 20-year-olds who had bought some of the stolen property from the boys in exchange for some cannabis.

All of the boys were from affluent middle-class families, the
kind of families in which 'this sort of thing is not meant to
happen'. At the start of the conference, the boys as well as
their parents sat as if frozen inside that pattern of thought:
this is not happening, this should not have happened, I
should not be here. On the other side of the room sat the
members of the family the boys had robbed. They were frozen
inside their fury. This had not been any old burglary: first
because it was a very, very wealthy family, and second because
one of the older sons in the family was a friend and a class-
mate of the boys who had robbed them.

When the officer in charge gave the victims of the crime
their chance to speak, a number of these boys went abruptly
from paralysis mode to violent coughing fits. The same happened to one of their fathers. When the time came for him
and the other parents to speak, they spoke eloquently about
their shame and their regret, their incomprehension and their
sorrow. They offered abject apologies, too, and although it
was clear from their voices that they blamed themselves for
what had happened (and clear from the expressions of the
robbed family that they held them responsible too) the first
five parents to speak could not quite bring themselves to
admit it.

It was the sixth parent who admitted looking back on the
previous year and realising how little time she had given her

son, who admitted thinking back over the days during which the robberies had happened, and seeing that there had been little signs that she had been too busy to pick up. 'They were little things. *Little* things,' she kept saying. Listening to her talk was like watching someone defrost. Suddenly her fingers could move once again. She pushed them through her hair over and over again, as if trying to get her brain to work. Although the other parents did not follow her out onto the limb, they too became more relaxed. It was as if she had said it for them. After she had broken the ice, said the unsayable, the other parents began to talk, just a little, about the future. As did their sons; as did the members of the family they had burgled. My guess is that their understanding of what had happened to them was not very much greater when they left the room than it had been when they arrived. But there was this sense that something had shifted, because now they had seen the people they most feared or most hated. The event was no longer a nightmare. It was awful, but it was real. They had looked at it, and now they could begin thinking about it – and by thinking, move forward.

I would not like to have been in their shoes. And had I been, I would not have liked the idea of being forced to participate in a restorative justice conference. But it was clear to me that it achieved a miracle, and it was clear too that this miracle could never have happened without the police being involved.

Again, a lot of the credit must go to the officer who ran the conference. He treated all those present with respect, and he gave them all an equal chance to speak. He kept control of the tensions in the room: there were only two angry outbursts, and both were short. He told me afterwards that he had come out of the 'hard end' of policing, 'things like public disturbances'. Doing this sort of work, he said, 'makes it easier to sleep at night'. The conferences were revelations for him, too:

they had challenged some of his most basic assumptions about policing – what it should be about and what it could do – and it had also made him look at the communities he served in a new light.

But contrast this with my third example, which comes from the opposite end of the parent business. The occasion was a very enlightened and well-meaning conference on improving services for fathers. Well attended by members of the relevant government policy units, it featured illuminating talks by family policy experts from the US and Australia as well as British experts.

Also present were a good number of men from grassroots fathers' groups. Although most of them came from deprived areas and many had little day-to-day contact with their children, their general attitude about fathering was positive. The ones who had been involved in their groups for a number of years were very articulate about their desire to be more consistent, more affectionate and less violent than their own fathers had been. The ones who were new to the experience were more tentative. For example, one man with nine children said his group had turned out to be 'much more interesting' than he'd expected. When I asked him what he got from it, he thought very carefully before saying, 'I think I never realised before that I was a father. Or that I could do things for my kids that made their life better.'

Most of the men had come to the conference in the hope that they could make a case for better funding to the relevant authorities. Perhaps I should say any funding, because mainly they had been able to obtain no funding whatsoever. But they did not get a chance to put their case to the full conference. Nor did they have the opportunity to call to account an academic who did speak to the conference about a survey she had conducted to find out why it was that fathers stayed away from existing services. One of the findings was that most men felt there was too much talk, and not enough football or DIY. At lunchtime, the men were grumbling about that a lot. 'It's not true,' they said. 'We can talk, and we like it, and we're good at it.' 'The problem,' said another, 'is they want us to talk the way *they* talk, and they're not going to give us any money until we agree to play their game.' The problem was inadvertently highlighted by the kind and well-meaning woman who did the summation at the end of the day. No one has worked harder for fathers than she has. If these men's groups ever do get public funding, they will have this person more than any other to thank. But the main lesson she asked her audience to draw from the conference was that 'we can work with fathers'. *We* can work with *them*.

The case for parental rights

There is a very good reason why the new family policies slip back so easily into the old conventions they are meant to replace. They do not give their citizen parents an equal role in their imagined partnership because they descend from a long political tradition in which people engaged in unpaid caring work had no political role whatsoever. The new policies might depart from the old thinking in significant ways, but the conception of the family as the bedrock of society, the thing underneath that needs to be managed from above, remains unchallenged. Starting from this vision of the family, even the most benevolent policies will be paternalistic in structure if not in spirit. They will assume parents who are not quite equipped to run their own lives and need careful guidance and management if they are to do their jobs properly. Even where they give importance to the conditions under which active parents work, they will allocate greater importance to their moral foundation. They will see any resistance to policy on the part of parents not as 'the sort of challenge that keeps a democracy democratic' but as recalcitrance. They will rarely see parents themselves as a source of creative energy, and never imagine policy from the parents' point of view.

But that's what we need if we really want that new partnership and the new morality. We need a framework that starts from the parents' point of view – a framework that allows us to ask not just what parents need and need to do but sees that they can be a source of ideas and creative energy – and then builds on those strengths. But there must be guarantees within that framework. Parents need rights.

Consider, for a moment, what it means to have rights in other areas of life. If you're an adult, and a functioning member of society, you're assumed to be reasonable, reliable and competent unless proved otherwise. But that does not mean that you are entitled to exercise your rights whenever your heart desires. If your rights are in conflict with other people's rights, then there are limits. And if you abuse your rights, you can lose them.

These obvious points get lost in discussions about parental rights. If I say that parents have rights, the first response is often a shudder, followed by a reminder about the legions of parents who don't deserve them. To talk about giving those parents rights is to suggest they we put their children in graver danger. But imagine applying that argument to other areas of life. Imagine saying that adults couldn't use banks any more because some of them were embezzlers. Imagine banning all drivers because some drivers drove when over the limit and ignored traffic lights. No one draws up a bill of rights using as their model a bank robber or a drunk driver. The model is always an ideal type, and the degree to which a human being can enjoy those rights depends on how hard he or she tries to live by the ideal. You can take rights away from people who act criminally or irresponsibly; but unless you give them rights, they cannot act at all.

Without rights, they have no way of making their voices heard in political debates. They have no way of making sure the state plays by the rules when it intervenes in their lives. They play no part either in the defining of those rules. Without rights, they cannot be citizens.

Michael Freeman, the children's rights advocate, says that such rights are important because possessing them is 'what is necessary to constitute personality. Those who lack rights are like slaves, means to another's ends, and never their own sovereigns.'[47] While it's true that adults do have rights as autonomous individuals, their rights as representatives of their families or their children are fast being eroded. This has happened as a direct consequence of the many panics about parenting, which have led to a growing consensus that parents have children for suspect reasons, and use them as extensions of their egos or for their private pleasure. Many people believe that curtailing parents' rights is wise, and state intervention in families is necessary, in order to keep parents from using their power over their children badly. But it also means that parents have less and less power to change their children's lives for the better.

It's to reverse this trend that I now propose to risk suggesting my own charter, a bill of parental rights for good-enough adults.

1   *The right to bear children.* The women's movement has made much of the right to refuse to have children. Reproductive freedom has always implied the right to have children as well, but this option has been less well

defended, partly because it seemed as if this right was
not at risk. But a quick look at the history of the family
planning movement shows that it has long been challenged. Poor women who have too many children have
always been problematic for the population control
movement. Ideas about who should be allowed to pro-
create freely and whose procreation should be curbed are
riddled with class and racial prejudices. And now, with
the arrival of genetic design technology, these prejudices
will have more room in which to play. Already, it is difficult for a mother to justify keeping a child whom
society views as too handicapped, and therefore expensive to care for. As our standards of infant excellence
'improve', we'll be redrawing the line between normal
and abnormal accordingly. If adults do not have the right
to bear children, they will have no way of challenging
the state's standards and will have to go along with them
even if they want to have the child that the state sees as
substandard.

As with all the other rights that follow, this right
comes with responsibilities. The most important are to
undertake to nurture, protect and educate your children,
and to be as responsive to their needs, and as attentive to
the way in which they express and define them, as their
age and your situation allows. But you can't take responsibility for children unless you first have the right to
bring them into the world.

2 *The right to raise children.* This is a right which parents
do have now, and that they need to make sure they keep,
as it is this right which the moral panics about bad parents have challenged most successfully. Parents should
be assumed to be competent unless proved otherwise.
Fathers who want to be involved in the raising of their

children should have the same rights and legal protections as mothers – both at home and in the workplace. At present, they often have full responsibilities but they do not have full rights. It should be clear from this that mothers and fathers often have conflicting interests, and conflicting rights: at the same time they have common interests too, and these are what we're looking at here, not the state of play between parents but between parents and the state.

3   *The right to create a home.* The American feminist bell hooks once said that while white, middle-class, university-educated feminists were fond of seeing motherhood as dehumanising, this has never been the view of poor black mothers. *They* have always worked, she said. It was at work that they were dehumanised. It was at home where they were able to make a life based on their own culture, and imbue it with their own meaning. That's what I mean by the right to create a home. To create a home for your children, you need a basic level of economic security. You need time. You need a house. And you need a front door you can close. You need privacy to create a home. If you have people barging in at all times, it isn't possible to keep the simplest routines going. Children might suffer authoritarian discipline, but that is not the same as saying that they benefit from parents who can exercise no authority at all. Interventions will always be necessary in some instances; but without any privacy at all, a home ceases to be a haven – as anyone who has ever lived in a totalitarian state can tell you.

4   *The right to informality.* The more the state becomes involved in the rearing of children, the more the subject of child-rearing belongs to the domain of expert

knowledge, the rearing of children becomes a skill like any other – something for which you must be trained, assessed and marked. There is nothing inherently wrong about formal child-rearing, and there is a lot that is inherently right about it; but it is important to insist on the right to draw from our tacit knowledge of informal child-rearing. This is a culture that has never been elaborated on paper, and that gets passed on from generation to generation through custom and practice – but this does not mean it is a stupid or entirely backward culture, either. It is a culture people reflect on, and argue about, and change according to their revised ideas of right and wrong when they go on to raise their own children. If we go along with this idea that child-rearing is something you can only learn at school, this other tradition will be devalued and eventually lost.

5   *The right to determine your own marital status*. Too often, discussions about divorce and cohabitation imply that people who choose not to marry, or not to stay married, do so out of immaturity, inconstancy and laziness. In so doing, they overlook the fact that these decisions often arise out of the conditions in which couples live, and out of disagreements about power that the larger society cannot help them with either, because the old consensus about the distribution of power inside marriage has broken down. There might be people who divorce lightly, but we must assume that most do not, and certainly the evidence suggests that life after divorce is easy for no one. Of course it's a good idea to proceed slowly, and to seek outside advice and support. But at the end of the day, people should be allowed the dignity of making their own decisions. If it were assumed that even divorcing and separating people knew it was easier to bring up

children in a two-parent family, then it would follow that they only take this step if there are serious problems. They shouldn't have to spell these out to the world to get 'excused' from selfishness. To advertise marriage problems in this way is unkind to the children involved.

And another thing – children shouldn't have to know all the details of their parents' marriage troubles. They do need to work out how to keep their ties with both parents, and avoid taking sides. Laws that regularise the involvement of non-resident parents, and that help them to keep in contact with their children, would be far more useful than laws to privilege marriage or impede divorce.

6   *The right to plan, choose, share and define care*. Without this right, the only parent who can provide proper care for a child is a dependant with a very reliable provider. With this right, a parent can vary a package of care according to a family's overall needs, can ensure that care is provided in a smooth and humane way, can reject care that he or she sees as dangerous or unsuitable and take steps to design a better form of care in its place. Where provision of care is piecemeal and patchy – in other words, in Britain – the right to plan, choose and share care gives a parent a starting point for arguing for better facilities, and also for family-friendly policies that allow them to plan for more time at home.

7   *The right to define support*. The standard way of defining support is from the top. But parents, families and communities should have the right to identify their own needs, define their own aims and put together their own plans. This is what happened, almost by accident, in Northern Ireland. The EU poured a lot of money into women's groups because of the community

networking they were doing that was so vital to the peace process. This allowed these groups to greatly enhance the networks in their own communities, too. And once they had that power base, they came up with more ideas for ways in which they could make life better in their neighbourhoods. So instead of waiting for the various large charities to come and offer pre-packaged help, they began to make their own plans and then go to those charities and tell them exactly what they needed. The charities later said that it had been a revelation to discover how much more effec-tively their money was spent in these areas once they established the habit of getting the neighbourhood net-works to make the first steps and then following their instructions. If parents had the right to define support, they could obtain support that was better tailored to their needs, and the needs of their communities, and also protect themselves against clumsy moralistic inter-ventions. It would also allow them to seek support that is confidential.

8 *The right to receive support.* This would give parents the right to demand that the state designs all the institu-tions that are meant to support them in such a way that they actually do support them. This right covers every-thing from maternity and paternity leave to mortgages and pension cover, sick leave for children's illnesses, and retraining schemes for parents who take long stretches of time off work to look after children. It also allows par-ents to ask for changes in the structure of the work day, not to mention the structure of careers and schools.

9 *The right to challenge intervention.* It doesn't matter how well-intended or benign a state policy is: if the people

who implement it are not accountable, and have the power to override the judgement of parents in all instances, then they have too much power. So a parent should be able to insist that all interventionists explain what they're doing and why; they should be accountable and their files should be open.

10   *The right to be consulted.* Ever since Victoria Gillick contested a young person's right to confidential family planning advice, a parent's right to be consulted has come to imply a parent's desire to obstruct a child's autonomy. But there are many instances in which a parent is actually trying to help a child become more autonomous; or needs to protect that child from things that most reasonable people would see as harmful to him; or needs to make sure that others who are responsible for him are not treating him unfairly or neglecting him. A parent can often be a child's best advocate, and so should insist on this right.

11   *The right to have an independent life.* Traditionally, parents who cared for their children were dependants. This 'freed' them to lead lives that may have looked selfless, but could never have happened unless someone else was paying for it. Today we can not afford that fiction any more. All parents must have the right to an independent life, even if they choose not to use it, firstly because they are not just parents but people with their own needs too, and secondly because if they have no access to an independent life, they will not be able to support their children.

12   *The right to represent your children's interests.* One of the most positive results of the children's rights movement has been the growing understanding that children's

voices are excluded from public discourse. To redress
this problem, there have been many efforts to seek out
children's views, both privately on confidential helplines
and publicly by including them in formal debates.
Charities and think tanks have published study after
study in which children have explained in their own
words what they think about their families, their
schools, their friends, what they see on television, what
they'd like to do and can't, what upsets them, and what
they can and cannot talk about with their parents. It
would not be right if they could not speak about their
own lives in public, just as it would not be right if only
parents had the right to speak for children in public.
But parents do know their children very well, and listen
to them very carefully too, and so they are often in a far
better position to see their needs early and then to represent those needs, and their larger interests, in public.
Speaking of which, a lot of these larger interests are far
too large for even the most brilliant child to understand.
No child should have to go to a meeting to fight the clo-
sure of a hospital or education cuts. A parent needs the
right to do it for him.

13   *The right to define the place of parents in society.* The first
      step is to move beyond this idea that parenting is some-
      thing that goes on in a box. It's only when you've left this
      illusion behind that you begin to see the numerous links
      your children have with other people, and the many
      others with whom you share responsibility for them.
      Once you see them, too, as people with rights, it is easier
      to identify where you have conflicts of interest and
      where you have common aims. Once that is done, it's
      easier to look at the material conditions under which
      people bring up children. You can begin to ask how

many of these horrible stories we've looked at in this book derive from moral failure alone, and how many stem from the low status of caring work and the appalling sacrifices so many parents make routinely, out of love as much as out of obligation, without anyone even noticing. You start to ask questions about how we treat parents as a group in this society, and to make connections between the way we treat parents and the way we treat people who do other forms of caring. You then begin to list all the types of care that go on in this country. You start to notice that most types of care are essential, not just for the smooth running of society but for all people who live in it, because no one is ever fully independent and autonomous. You remember that we're all heavily dependent on other people when we're very young, and very old, and very ill; and that even when we're at the top of our form, we still have to depend on countless others if we are to meet our basic needs.

You then begin to see how the recent changes in the economy have ravaged unpaid carers and the people who depend on them. You notice, too, that some things have not changed at all: that even where care is paid the pay is almost always at the low end of the scale. You notice, too, that the best-off in society are the individuals who get the most and the best care. And because privilege does have a way of looking after itself, you begin to wonder if the scapegoating, moralising, downgrading, underpaying and exclusion of parents and other carers might not be entirely in good faith, might be to justify that privilege and help maintain it. It's a depressing thought; but once you've entertained it, it becomes possible to imagine a world in which this trick of privilege fails to fool anyone, and in which parents and other carers begin to have a say in the way their work is ordered, and valued, and properly supported. Which brings us to the last right:

14 *The right to represent the larger interests of parents and other carers, and to explore the large ethical and political dilemmas of domestic life, in the political arena.* If I've made nothing else clear in this book, at least I hope I have established that some of the greatest political questions of the new century are the issues that are playing themselves out in the 'haven' of the home. Once we stop blaming them on parents, or expecting parents to solve them privately, without bothering the grown-ups, or dismissing them as domestic – and therefore technical – matters, we can give them the attention and discussion they deserve.

But why bother to have children at all?

As I think back on the stories I've raked through in this book, there is one other sentence that I can not get out of my head: Deborah Eappen, saying of Louise Woodward, 'I hope she never has children. *I hope she never knows that joy.*' I always hear it as if spoken by Medea, as a curse. But every time I hear it, I wonder, how can *not* knowing that joy be a curse if you don't even know it's a joy in the first place? Why would anyone who has no inkling about the joy have any regrets at all?

Ask me if I have any regrets about having children, and you might as well be asking me if I've ever considered living without limbs, or what I imagine my life might have been like if I'd never learned to read. Children are too much part of my life; I can't imagine being without them. But to ask why people bother to have children is a very good question; and with the birth rate in this country dropping at the rate it is, it might become a question we start taking seriously.

In a society that thinks in terms of objectives and outcomes, costs and benefits, there *is* no good reason to spend twenty or thirty years of your life in service to people who will never repay you for your efforts, and may never thank you. However, in a society that looks for hidden motives in all apparent acts of altruism, there are many bad reasons. People have children because their lives are empty; they are trying to patch up a hopeless marriage when really they should let the poor man go; they are seeking status; they want a little doll to play house with; they need someone small and vulnerable to need them; a child will validate them, affirm their masculinity, advertise their femininity, give them an inflated idea of their own importance.

In a society where you count for nothing unless you can stand on your own two feet, there are many good reasons *not* to have children. You can look forward to an uninterrupted work life; you will actually be able to support yourself on what you earn; you can look at *Time Out* without asking yourself what happened to those days when a film you had always wanted to see was showing around the corner, and throw on your coat to go and see if there were still tickets. You can sleep late on Sundays. When you book holidays, you don't have to multiply the bargain air-fares by four or five or six. When you arrive at your destination, you can sunbathe all day without ever having to get up and buy someone an ice cream. You never have to reach into your handbag to find out what that strange bulge is and pull out a leg that once belonged to a Civil War Nurse Barbie. You have time to write thank-you notes and remember old friends. When you pick up your address book, you do not find it decorated with hearts and stick figures. When you need a pen, the first place you look is not under the sofa cushions, or behind the toothbrush glass, or inside your shoe.

It is easy to understand why more and more people are coming to see how foolish it is to disrupt the gracious rhythms of adult life, and deciding not to have any children at all. My own life would have been a lot easier if I had followed in their footsteps. I was never under any pressure to become a mother. I have never been able to explain, to myself or anyone else, why I did have children, why I ended up having *four* children. I don't remember agonising the way you're meant to do about all the implications of this momentous decision. All I remember is longing for a child, and then coming to understand – but only at his birth – what an amazing thing it was to have the power to create another life.

At that point, I was still under the delusion that I would also have the power to shape him into just the sort of child I wanted. I never gave up trying, but if I had to say what I've treasured most about the times I've had with all four of my children, it's been the things they surprised me with, the things they did or said or thought up or discovered by themselves. When my son was one, for example, and decided the way to eat bread and jam was with the jam on the underside because that way it was easier to lick it off. When he was three and asked me the first question I couldn't answer, about why there was a universe. When my eldest daughter woke up early one morning when she was five (or was it six), took my cheque-book out of my handbag and wrote me a cheque for a million pounds. When she wrapped up all my jewellery in the pages of a typescript I was printing out and gave it all back to me. When my two little daughters decorated my bedroom with two hundred plastic animals, and positioned them in such a way that they were all facing the television set. When they learned how to count to ten in Turkish. When they taught themselves the words to 'Norwegian Wood'. When they tried and failed to teach me sign language. When I took them to a village in Spain, and they kept themselves amused by counting the things they saw and couldn't understand.

They called these things 'the mysteries'. From the days when they were born, they themselves have been mysteries to me. No two of my children have ever held a cup in the same way, had the same way of walking, the same voice, or the same way of singing, thinking, laughing, or seeing the world. Bringing them up has mostly meant watching them become themselves. It's a terrible mistake to think that parents are the wise ones, and children their blank slates. I've learned as much about life from watching my children grow as they have ever learned from watching me.

I've agonised as any parent about whether or not I have brought them up to have the right kind of manners, and the right set of values, and the right attitude to work, life and other people. I entertain the usual vain hope that they will all turn into thoughtful, talented, happy and dependable adults. I indulge in as many impossible fantasies as any parent about the amazing things they might do for mankind one day, thus proving to the world that I was a much better parent than they ever imagined. But there is one ambition I am pretty sure I never had. I don't think I ever sat down with their fathers and said, 'Here's an idea. Let's spend the next twenty years or so raising children according to government standards. Let's become a building block of society, and turn out a host of responsible citizens. Let's make sure they grow up knowing that really *really* good citizens should always do what the state tells them to do, and never question it.'

Governments cannot help but look at children and childhood in instrumental terms. And so when they regulate and legislate for childhood, they will inevitably resort to the language of the factory. Just as inevitably, when children and young people don't behave in a way that is convenient for them, they are going to see this behaviour as anti-social. The problems begin when there is no one out there to challenge this view of things, or to suggest that it is not the only valid interpretation of events.

The worst thing about our current panic concerning parents and parenthood is that it makes state interventions seem necessary. We're failing our children, and our families are disintegrating, so someone must step in and restore the moral order. What's broken must be fixed.

But there have always been parents who fail their children, and there always will be. So long as most parents operate in conditions as appalling as they are today, we can be pretty sure there will continue to be many, many of them who fail their children. Efforts to police and lecture them, name and shame them, may make those parents feel very bad, and the rest of us feel at least temporarily superior, but it won't solve the problems that pushed such parents over the edge. To go along with a government that indulges in such activities is to allow that government to avoid dealing with the problems that cause all families in this country to suffer.

But this is not to say that the scapegoating of parents is a clever government plot. It's something in our culture, something we all seem to take great pleasure in – a way of confirming to ourselves that actually, despite all the changes we've gone through over the past decades, most of us still have the same values, or at least the same understanding of what we've almost lost. Scapegoating parents is a form of moral shorthand. Look at them, we say. Is this what the world is coming to? Maybe it won't be if we punish them for their sins.

To imply that a parent fails because of lapsed morals is to imply that there's an easy solution. You don't have to solve poverty, or redesign your employment policy, or try to figure out how you factor in unpaid work when planning a market economy. All you have to do is give people lessons, and then more lessons. If they still don't learn, all they deserve is a lecture and a stiff fine. I can see the attraction of this argument. What I can't understand is how anybody could seriously believe it. You have only to use your eyes and think for a moment to see that there is always more to it than that.

This brings me to the one thing I really do hope I have taught my children. I hope I've taught them that believing in fairy-stories just because they're comforting can be a dangerous enterprise. I hope I've taught them that while it is sometimes inconvenient to stop and use your eyes and think, and ask awkward questions, this is also what makes a democracy stay democratic, a society ethical and a conscience clear. I hope I've taught them that, because it was from them I rediscovered the importance of asking inconvenient questions – because that is what children do. They ask things they're not meant to do, at times when they're meant to be doing something else. They stubbornly insist on seeing life as a mystery to explore instead of a grim plan they must honour. They revel in the little things that adults forget to look at. They show their emotions, even to the point of showing pleasure when they see themselves in the mirror. They look forward to their birthdays. Even when they refuse to eat their vegetables, they grow. They ask, 'Why?' These are just a few of the miracles they perform for their parents, and that is why even today, with things so grim and getting daily grimmer, parents still talk about life with children as a joy. I hope my children will be able to know this joy themselves when they grow up, and I hope that then as now they will keep on stopping and looking and asking those inconvenient questions. It is for them that I have written this very inconvenient book.

Bibliography

Beauvoir, Simone de, *The Second Sex*, Everyman's Library, London, 1993.

Beck, Ulrich and Beck-Gernsheim, Elisabeth, *The Normal Chaos of Love*, Polity Press, London, 1995.

Benn, Melissa, *Madonna and Child*, Jonathan Cape, London, 1998.

Brannen, Julia et al, *Employment and Family Life, A review of research in the UK 1980–94*, Dept of Employment, London, 1994.

Bright Futures, Mental Health Foundation, London, 1999.

Burges, Louie and Brown, Mark, *Single Lone Mothers: Problems, prospects and policies*, Family Policy Studies Centre, London, 1995.

Burgess, Adrienne, *Fatherhood Reclaimed: the Making of the Modern Father*, Vermillion, London, 1997.

Buxton, Jayne, *Ending the Mother War, Starting the Workplace Revolution*, Macmillan, London, 1998.

Cockett, Monica and Tripp, John, *The Exeter Family Study: Family breakdown and its impact on children*, Exeter University Press, 1996.

Cohen, Cathy J. et al (eds), *Women Transforming Politics: An Alternative Reader*, New York University Press, New York, 1997.

Craig, T.K.J. et al, *Off to a Bad Start: a longitudinal study of homeless young people in London*, Mental Health Foundation, London, 1996.

Daly, Martin and Wilson, Margo, *The Truth About Cinderella; A Darwinian View of Parental Love*, Weidenfeld and Nicolson, London, 1998.

Donzelot, Jacques, *The Policing of Families*, tr. Robert Hurley, Johns Hopkins, Baltimore, 1997.

Drew, Eileen et al (eds), *Women, Work, and the Family in Europe*, Routledge, London, 1998.

Eekelaar, John and Sarcevic, Petar, *Parenthood in Modern Society: Legal and Social Issues for the Twenty-first Century*, Martinus Nijhoff Publishers, Dordrecht, 1993.

Etzioni, Amitai, *The New Golden Rule: Community and Morality in a Democratic Society*, Profile Books, London, 1997.

———, *The Spirit of Community: Rights, Responsibilities, and the Communitarian Agenda*, Fontana Press, London, 1995.

Ferri, Elsa and Smith, Kate, *Parenting in the 1990s*, FPRC, London, 1996.

———, *Step-parenting in the 1990s*, FPRC, London, 1998.

Forward, Dr Susan, *Toxic Parents: Overcoming Their Hurtful Legacy and Reclaiming Your Life*, Bantam Books, New York, 1990.

Franks, Suzanne, *Having None of It: Women, Men and the Future of Work*, Granta Books, London, 1998.

Freely, Maureen and Pyper, Dr Celia, *Pandora's Clock*, Heinemann, London, 1993.

Freeman, Michael and Veerman, Phillip (eds), *The Ideologies of Children's Rights*, Martinus Nijhoff Publishers, Dordrecht, 1992.

Furedi, Frank, *The Culture of Fear: Risk-taking and the Morality of Low Expectation*, Cassell, London, 1997.

Galinksy, Ellen, *Ask the Children*, William Morrow, New York, 1999.

Gardiner, Jean, *Gender, Care and Economics*, Macmillan, London, 1996.

Graham, Philip and Hughes, Carol, *So Young So Sad So Listen*, Royal College of Psychiatrists, Gaskell, London, 1995.

Gutman, Amy and Thompson, Dennis, *Democracy and Disagreement: Why Moral Conflict Cannot be Avoided in Politics, and What Should Be Done About It*, Belknap, Harvard University Press, Cambridge, Mass., 1996.

Hewitt, Patricia and Leach, Penelope, *Social Justice, Children and Families*, Commission on Social Justice, IPPR, London, 1993.

Hewlett, Sylvia Ann and West, Cornel, *The War Against Parents: What We Can Do for America's Beleaguered Moms and Dads*, Houghton Mifflin, New York, 1998.

Higonnet, Anne, *Pictures of Innocence*, Thames and Hudson, London, 1998.

Hochschild, Arlie, *The Time Bind*, Metropolitan Books, New York, 1997.

Jones, Gill, *Family Support for Young People*, FPRC, London, 1995.

Joshi, Heather, et al, *Dependence and Independence in the Finances of Women aged 33*, FPRC, London, 1995.

Kaminer, Wendy, *I'm Dysfunctional, You're Dysfunctional: The Recovery Movement and Other Self-Help Fashions*, Vintage, 1993.

Kurtz, Sarrina, *Treating Children Well*, Mental Health Foundation, London, 1996.

Levitas, Ruth, *The Inclusive Society?: Social Exclusion and New Labour*, Macmillan Press, London, 1998.

Lister, Ruth, *Citizenship: Feminist Perspectives*, Macmillan, London, 1997.

Luker, Kristin, *Dubious Conceptions: The Politics of Teenage Pregnancy*, Harvard University Press, Cambridge, Mass., 1996.

———, *Abortion and the Politics of Motherhood*, University of California Press, Berkeley, 1984.

Makins, Virginia, *The Invisible Children: Nipping Failure in the Bud*, National Pyramid Trust, David Fulton Pubs, London, 1997.

McGlone, Francis et al, *Families and Kinship*, FPRC, London, 1998.

Millar, Jane and Warman, Andrea, *Family Obligations in Europe*, FPRC, 1996.

Miller, Alice, *Thou Shalt Not be Aware: Society's Betrayal of the Child*, Pluto Press, London, 1998.

Morgan, Patricia, *Who Needs Parents? The Effects of Childcare and Early Education on Children in Britain and the USA*, IEA Health and Welfare Unit, London, 1996.

Morrow, Virginia, *Understanding Families: Children's Perspectives*, National Children's Bureau and the Joseph Rowntree Foundation, London, 1998.

Naples, Nancy A., *Grassroots Warriors: Activist Mothering, Community Work, and the War on Poverty*, Routledge, London, 1997.

Phillips, Melanie, *The Sex-Change Society,* Social Market Foundation, London 1999

Popenoe, David et al, *Promises to Keep: Decline and Renewal of Marriage in America*, Rowman and Littlefield, Maryland, 1996.

Rapoport, R. and Bailyn, L., *Relinking Life and Work: Toward a Better Future*, Ford Foundation, New York, 1996.

Robertson, A.F., *Beyond the Family: The Social Organization of Human Reproduction*, Polity, Cambridge, 1991.

Ruddick, Sarah, *Maternal Thinking: Towards a Politics of Peace*, Women's Press, London, 1989.

Samuels, A., 'The good-enough father of either sex' in *Feminism and Psychology*, Sage, 1995.

Sennett, Richard, *The Corrosion of Character*, Norton, New York, 1998.

Showalter, Elaine, *Hystories*, Picador, London, 1997.

Simons, John (ed.), *High Divorce Rates: The State of the Evidence on Reasons and Remedies*, One Plus One Marriage and Partnership Research, Vols 1 and 2, London, 1999.

Smith, Celia and Pugh, Gillian, *Learning to be a Parent: a survey of group-based parenting programmes*, FPRC, London, 1996.

Smith, Joan, et al, *The Family Background of Homeless Young People*, FPRC, London, 1998.

Speak, Suzanne et al, *Young Single Fathers: participation in fatherhood – barriers and bridges*, FPRC, London, Dec 1997.

Supporting Families, Ministerial Group on the Family, The Law and Children's Rights, London, 1998.

Tronto, Joan, *Moral Boundaries: A Political Argument for an Ethic of Care*, Routledge, London, 1993.

Utting, David (ed.), *Children's Services Now and in the Future*, National Children's Bureau and Joseph Rowntree Foundation, London, 1998.

Varma, Ved, *Violence in Children and Adolescents*, Jessica Kingsley Publishers, London, 1997.

Waring, Marilyn, *If Women Counted*, Macmillan, London, 1989.

———, *Three Masquerades: Essays on Equality, Work and Human Rights*, Auckland University Press, Auckland, 1996.

Webster, R. *The Great Children's Home Panic*, The Orwell Press, Oxford, 1998.

Whitehead, Barbara Dafoe, *The Divorce Culture*, Alfred Knopf, New York, 1996.

Notes

1   The Basic Plots

1   *Daily Mail*, 2.7.94.
2   *Daily Mail*, 19.7.94.
3   Ibid.
4   *Daily Mail*, 3.7.94.
5   *Beyond the Family*, p. 10.
6   Ibid, p. 18.
7   Higonnet Anne, *Pictures of Innocence*, p. 213.
8   *Daily Mail*, 3.7.94.
9   Ibid.
10 *Daily Mail*, 2.7.94.
11 *Daily Mail*, 3.7.94.
12 Ibid.
13 *Daily Mail*, 19.7.94.
14 *Times*, 10.12.94.
15 Ibid.
16 *Daily Mail*, 19.7.94.
17 *Daily Mail*, 18.7.98.
18 *Sunday Times*, 29.6.97.
19 *Daily Mail*, 16.3.94.
20 Robertson, A.F., *Beyond the Family*, p. 19.

21   Ibid, p. 9.
22   Ibid, p. 17.
23   Ibid, pp. 70–72.
24   *Times*, 14.1.97.
25   *Times*, 30.6.98.
26   *Observer*, 13.12.98; *Times* and *Daily Mail*, 15.12.98.
27   Interview with author.
28   *News of the World*, 11.8.96.
29   *News of the World*, 18.8.96.
30   Ibid.
31   *Sun*, 12.8.96.
32   *News of the World*, 11.8.96.
33   *Mail on Sunday*, 11.8.96.
34   *Sun*, 12.8.96.
35   *Guardian*, 13.8.96.
36   *Times*, 12.8.96.
37   *Daily Telegraph*, 12.8.96.
38   *Sunday Express*, 25.8.96.
39   *Sunday Express*, 25.8.96.
40   Headlines from *Guardian*, *Daily Telegraph* and *The Times*, 18.5.99, and from *Daily Telegraph*, 15.6.99.
41   *Guardian*, 16.6.99.
42   *Guardian*, 6.8.99.
43   *Guardian*, 16.9.99.
44   *Daily Mail*, 2.10.99.
45   Coverage of original trial in *The Times*, 11.2.97, 4.10.97–1.11.97.
46   Ibid.
47   Ibid.
48   *Times*, 10.10.97.
49   *Times*, 18.11.97.
50   *Times*, 10.10.97.
51   *Sunday Times*, 1.11.97.
52   *Times*, 10.10.97.
53   *Times*, 31.10.97.
54   *Guardian*, 1.11.97.
55   *Times*, 11.3.97.

56   Ibid.
57   *Guardian*, 4.11.97.
58   *Times*, 5.11.97.
59   *Sunday Times*, 2.11.97
60   *Guardian*, 4.11.97.
61   *Times*, 1.11.97.
62   Ibid.
63   Ibid.
64   *Times*, 6.11.97.
65   *Guardian*, 6.11.97.
66   *Guardian*, 9.11.97.
67   *Times*, 11.11.97.
68   Ibid.
69   Ibid.
70   Ibid.
71   *Guardian*, 10.6.98.
72   *Guardian*, 15.6.98.
73   *Times*, 18.6.98.
74   *Times*, 18.11.97.
75   *Times*, 16.11.97.
76   *Times*, 18.11.97.
77   *Times*, 23.6.98.
78   *Times*, 13.11.97.
79   *Guardian*, 11.11.97.
80   *Times*, 12.11.97.

2   The Cast of Characters

1   *Daily Mail*, 10.12.98.
2   *Guardian*, 26.9.97.
3   See Buxton, Jayne, *Ending the Mother Wars*.
4   See Franks, Suzanne, *Having None of It*.
5   Benn, Melissa, *Madonna and Child: Towards a New Politics of Motherhood*, pp. 244–254.
6   See Galinsky, Ellen, *Ask the Children: What America's Children Really Think of Working Parents*, p. 225.

7 *Relinking Life and Work: Toward a Better Future*, New York, Ford Foundation, 1996.
8 See Hochschild, Arlie, *The Time Bind*.
9 *Observer*, 4.7.99.
10 Waring, Marilyn, *If Women Counted*.
11 *Times*, 11.12.97.
12 Family Policy Studies Centre, p. 5 on single lone mothers.
13 Ibid, p. 14.
14 *Single Lone Mothers: Problems, prospects and policies*, FPSC, by Louie Burghes with Mark Brown, November 1995, p. 19.
15 Speak, Suzanne et al, *Young Single Fathers: participation in fatherhood – barriers and bridges*, p. 36.
16 *Guardian*, 19.9.97.
17 *Observer*, 27.12.98.
18 Press release, Royal Society for the Encouragement of Arts, Manufacturers and Commerce, Feb. 1996.
19 Burgess, *Fatherhood Reclaimed*, pp. 214–15.
20 *Guardian*, 10.3.98.
21 *Daily Telegraph*, 3.7.98.
22 *Guardian*, 26.8.98.
23 *Guardian*, 27.11.98.
24 Popenoe, *Promises to Keep*.
25 Phillips, Melanie, *The sex change state*.
26 *Guardian*, 24.11.98.
27 *Guardian*, 24.4.98.
28 *Guardian*, 15.11.97.
29 *Daily Mail* and *Daily Express*, 10.12.98.
30 *Daily Mail*, 21.10.98.
31 Child Abuse and Stepfamilies Factfile 4, 1996. The National Stepfamily Association, London.
32 *The Family Background of Young People*, FPSC, p. 32.
33 Daly, Martin and Wilson, Margo, *The Truth about Cinderella*.
34 Prosser, J. *Child Abuse Investigations – the Families' Perspective*, Parents Against Injustice.
35 *Daily Telegraph*, 23.10.96.
36 Furedi, Frank, *The Culture of Fear*, p. 99.
37 Webster, Richard, 'The Great Children's Home Panic'.

38 *Guardian*, 18.10.97.
39 Ibid.
40 *Guardian*, 24.4.98; and *Times*, 27.4.98.
41 *Guardian*, 25.4.98.
42 Home Office, 4.5.99.
43 *Families for Freedom*. Child Safety Bulletin, 4.6.97.
44 Ibid.
45 Ibid.
46 Ibid.
47 *Guardian*, 25.4.98.
48 *Guardian*, 17.10.97.
49 Samuels, Andrew, 'Men under scrutiny' in *Psychological Perspective*, issue 26, 1992; 'The good-enough father of either sex' in *Feminism and Psychology*, Sage, 1995.

3   The Shaky Foundations

1 *Guardian*, 28.10.97.
2 *Times*, 28.10.97; *Guardian*, 28.10.97.
3 *Guardian*, 10.12.99.
4 *Guardian*, 28.10.97.
5 *Times*, 28.10.97.
6 *Guardian*, 15.10.97.
7 *Daily Telegraph*, 26.11.98.
8 *Guardian*, 25.11.98.
9 *Daily Telegraph*, 5.9.95.
10 *Daily Telegraph*, 28.11.95.
11 *Daily Telegraph*, 21.6.95.
12 *Independent*, 1.8.98.
13 *Daily Mail* and *Guardian*, 15.12.98.
14 *Independent*, 1.8.98.
15 *Guardian*, 7.1.99.
16 Ibid, 19.7.99.
17 Ibid, 13.1.99.
18 McGillivray in Freeman (ed) *The Ideologies of Children's Rights*, p. 226.

19 Ibid.
20 *Guardian*, 28.5.99.
21 Ibid, 17.6.99.
22 *Independent*, 8.1.94.
23 Ibid.
24 Ibid.
25 Ibid, 10.9.94.
26 Ibid, 10.2.94.
27 Ibid, 7.2.94.
28 *Daily Telegraph*, 23.10.95.
29 Ibid, 30.11.95.
30 *Times* Index, 1994, 356,7.
31 *One Plus One*, Socio-Demographic Predictors of Divorce by Lynda Clarke and Ann Berrington (v).
32 Mansfield, Penny et al (eds), *One Plus One*, 'What policy developments would be most likely to secure improvements in marital stability?' p 18.
33 See Whitehead Dafoe, Barbara, *The Divorce Culture*.
34 *Exeter Family Study*, p. 63.
35 Beck and Beck-Gersheim, *The Normal Chaos of Love*, pp. 147–50.
36 *Daily Express*, 5.1.99.
37 *Daily Mail*, 5.1.99.
38 Interview with author, 28.2.98.
39 Freeman (ed) *The Ideologies of Children's Rights*, 'Reconstructing child abuse', p. 214.
40 Wilson, Peter, interview with author, 2.98.
41 Figures for mental illness in children, are from Graham, P., *So Young So Sad So Listen*.
42 Interview with author.
43 Interview with Jane Whittington.
44 Parenting Forum, 'Why classes must be voluntary', The Parenting Forum newsletter, Spring 1999, Briefing Sheet No. 13, p. 3.
45 Interview with author.
46 *Bright Futures*, pp. 9–11.
47 *Guardian*, 1.5.98.

48 *Daily Telegraph*, 5.1.98.
49 *Daily Telegraph*, 5.7.98.
50 *Daily Telegraph*, 20.7.98.
51 *Daily Telegraph*, 18. 12. 98.
52 *Daily Mail*, 15.12.98.
53 *Guardian*, 12.12.98.
54 *Daily Telegraph*, 11.8.97.
55 Family Policy Studies Centre – Family Briefing p. 9, September 1999: Teenage Pregnancy and the Family, p. 7.
56 Mental Health Foundation Briefing Paper 1, 'Suicide and deliberate self-harm: the fundamental facts', 1.6.97.
57 The Work–life Research Centre, Institute of Education, University of London, London 1998.
58 Jones, Gill, 'Family Support for Young People', FPSC, p. 6.
59 Ibid.
60 *Daily Telegraph*, 27.10.98.
61 *Daily Mail*, 24.2.99.
62 *Daily Mail*, 15.12.98.
63 *Daily Telegraph*, 13.10.95.
64 *Daily Telegraph*, 18.1.96.
65 *Daily Telegraph*, 15.11.97.
66 *Daily Telegraph*, 4.1.98.
67 *Daily Telegraph*, 9.8.97.

4   The New Morality

1 *Daily Telegraph*, 18.10.96.
2 *Times*, 9.12.95.
3 *Daily Telegraph*, 18.10.96.
4 *Times*, 9.12.95.
5 *Times*, 11.12.95.
6 *Daily Telegraph*, 11.12.95.
7 *Times*, 11.12.95.
8 Ibid.
9 *Sunday Telegraph*, 17.12.95.
10 *Daily Telegraph*, 18.10.96.

11 *Daily Telegraph*, 23.10.96.
12 *Daily Telegraph*, 30.10.96
13 *Daily Telegraph*, 6.11.96.
14 *Times*, 9.12.96.
15 *Daily Telegraph*, 14.1.97.
16 *Times*, 3.1.98.
17 Ibid.
18 Ibid.
19 Ibid.
20 Ibid.
21 *Supporting Families*, p. 5.
22 Ibid.
23 *Supporting Families*, p. 4.
24 Ibid.
25 Ibid.
26 Katherine Bramwell at FPSC consultation.
27 *Sunday Times*, 5.1.98.
28 *Sunday Telegraph*, 5.1.98.
29 *Sunday Times*, 5.1.98.
30 *Sunday Times*, 5.1.98.
31 *Supporting Families*, p. 7.
32 Ibid, p. 11.
33 Ibid, p. 43.
34 Ibid.
35 Ibid, p. 42.
36 Ibid, p. 13.
37 Ibid, p. 11.
38 Ibid, p. 7.
39 Ibid, p. 42.
40 Ibid.
41 Tronto, Joan, *Moral Boundaries*, p. 145.
42 Ibid, p. 137.
43 Ibid, see Chs 4 and 5.
44 Ibid, p. 111.
45 Ibid, p. 135.
46 *Supporting Families*, FPSC Briefing Paper 11, p. 11, June 1999.
47 Freeman, Michael, *The Ideologies of Children's Rights*, p. 30.